The
Native People
of Alaska

Traditional living in a northern land

FOURTH EDITION

Steve J. Langdon

Greatland Graphics
Anchorage, Alaska

Acknowledgements

Many people have aided in the preparation of this book.

First I would like to thank all the Native people who have educated me and welcomed me into their homes in various parts of Alaska during the past three decades. It is my hope that this book will contribute to a wider appreciation of their traditional culture and present aspirations.

I have learned much about Alaska archeology from conversations with Doug Veltre, Bill Workman and David Yesner, archeological colleagues in the Anthropology Department of the University of Alaska-Anchorage.

Thanks also to Diane Brenner of the Anchorage Museum of History and Art for her assistance in identifying many of the photos which appear in this book and to Edward Bovy for his enthusiasm and editorial assistance.

Finally, a special thanks to Dr. Sven Haakanson and Patrick Saltonstall for their assistance with Alutiiq topics and images added to the fourth edition. I am responsible for any errors and interpretations presented in this book.

A portion of the author's proceeds from this book will be directed to Alaska Native organizations working to maintain traditional values, self-determination and ancestral lands for future generations of Alaska Natives.

S. L.

Notes on photos and illustrations
Most of the photos and illustrations in this book are 100 to 130 years old and were chosen to portray traditional life in Alaska before the arrival of modern conveniences.

The Native People of Alaska
©2002 Greatland Graphics
10 9 8 7 6 5 4 3 2 1

Original Library of Congress card catalogue number 92-074225
Fourth edition, 2002

Available by mail for $9.95 each plus $3 shipping/handling from:
    Greatland Graphics
    P. O. Box 100333
    Anchorage, Alaska 99510-0333
    www.alaskacalendars.com

Edit and design
Edward Bovy

Illustrations
Kathy Kiefer (pp. 24, 52), Kim Mincer (p. 32); additional illustrations from *Alaska and Its Resources* by William Dall (1870), *The Eskimo About Bering Strait* by Edward Nelson (1889), and the Harriman Alaska Expedition reports (1899).

Cartography
Jim Green

Front cover
Inupiat woman and child, 1906. The young mother in the photo is Abatnia Koruk, an Inupiat from King Island. She died a few years after the photo was taken, probably around 1918. Abatnia was likely a victim of the flu that took the lives of many Alaska Natives that year but she lives on in the body and mind of her granddaughter whose mother is the baby pictured here. (B. B. Dobbs Collection, Alaska State Library)

Facing page
Eskimo berry pickers, Nome, about 1910. (Anchorage Museum of History and Art B90.28.192)

Contents

CHAPTER 1

Introduction

Alaska, the great northwestern sub-continent of North America, is home to a unique and diverse group of aboriginal people. This book is an introduction to their culture and history.

Alaska's indigenous people, who are jointly called Alaska Natives, can be divided into six major groupings: Unangan/Aleut, Sugpiaq/Alutiiq (Pacific Eskimos), Yupiit (Bering Sea Eskimos), Inupiat (Northern Eskimos), Athabaskans (Interior Indians) and Tlingit and Haida (Southeast Coastal Indians). These groupings are based on broad cultural and linguistic similarities of peoples living contiguously in different regions of Alaska. They do not represent political or tribal units nor are they the units Native people have traditionally used to define themselves.

At the time of contact with Russian explorers in the mid-18th century, Alaska was occupied by approximately 80,000 indigenous people. The phrase "time of contact" means the earliest time when a Native group had significant direct interaction with Europeans. This time varied for different parts of Alaska; therefore Alaskan Native groups have had somewhat different historical experiences through their contact with Europeans and Americans.

Time of Contact for Alaskan Native Groups	
Unangan/Aleut	1750-1780
Pacific Eskimo	1760-1790
Bering Sea Eskimo	1780-1840
Southeast Coastal Indians	1785-1800
Interior Indians	1800-1870
Northern Eskimo	1850-1870

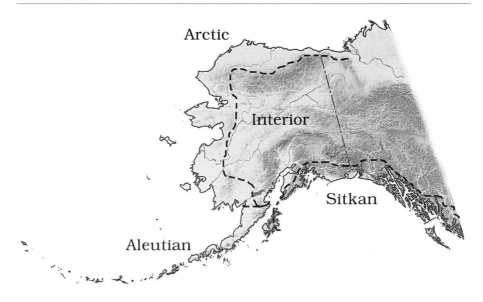

Alaska Environments

Alaska's huge landmass includes a number of diverse environments. The 533,000 square miles of Alaska are spread over nearly 20 degrees of latitude. Alaska is bound on three sides by water; its total coastline of 33,000 miles is as long as that of the rest of the United States. It is a land of harsh extremes from 250 inches of rainfall annually, to —80° F in the dead of winter, to howling gales with winds in excess of 100 knots. For those living above the Arctic Circle (66°33' N), there are days in the summer when the sun doesn't go down and nights in the winter when the sun doesn't rise.

But Alaska is blessed with abundant fish and wildlife which, with knowledge and care, can provide for many people. Many migratory species travel to Alaska in the summer to give birth to their offspring, making this season extremely vital for food production. Marine resources are especially abundant in the Bering Sea while Alaska's two major rivers, the Yukon and Kuskokwim, drain thousands of square miles of interior Alaska, providing habitat for many species of fish.

There are four major environments in Alaska where climatic conditions, flora and fauna are similar. Northeast from Kodiak Island and eastward to Southeast Alaska is the *Sitkan Zone*, a temperate rain forest where stands of Sitka spruce, cedar and hemlock form towering and impenetrable forests. The climate is mild and damp due to the influence of the warm Japanese Current from the tropics. There is relatively little seasonal variation across the Gulf of Alaska with winter temperatures rarely falling below freezing and summer temperatures rarely rising above 60°F.

The *Aleutian Zone* extends from central Kodiak Island to the tip of the Aleutians (including parts of the Alaska Peninsula), long grasses and shrubs are the major flora.

Extending in a two-hundred-mile-wide band around the western and northern coast of Alaska from Bristol Bay to the Canadian border is the *Arctic Zone*. Cold winters and cool summers are characteristic with the northern regions experiencing a more intense winter cold than the southern regions. *Tundra*, composed of ground-hugging flora such as mosses, lichens, sedges and shrubs, with few or no trees, is found throughout the Arctic.

The fourth Alaskan environment is the *Interior Zone* which lies south of the Brooks Range, north of the Alaska Range and east of the coastal strip of the Arctic environment. It is dominated by the Yukon River whose many tributaries drain the interior. Cold winters, with temperatures frequently below -50°F are offset by short, hot summers with temperatures occasionally above 90°F, thunderstorms and forest fires. The *boreal forest*, consisting of relatively small specimens of white and black spruce, alder, birch and aspen, covers most of the rolling hills characteristic of interior terrain. Immense, marshy flatlands, prime habitat for waterfowl, are found in bottomlands of many of the rivers.

The oceanic zones of Alaska as defined by the fish and animal populations that occupy them are the Gulf of Alaska (southern) and Arctic (northern) that are separated by the Alaska Peninsula and Aleutian Islands. The Gulf of Alaska is essentially ice free while the Bering and Chukchi Seas and Arctic Ocean that comprise the Arctic zone are seasonally covered with a combination of pack ice that advances from the north in the fall and shore fast ice that builds outward from the coast.

There are major differences in the marine mammal species found in each zone. Harbor seals, sea otters and Steller sea lions are found in the Gulf of Alaska and rarely north of the Aleutian Islands. Walrus, beluga whales (Cook Inlet's population are an exception), bearded, spotted and ringed seal, by contrast, are found in the Arctic zone but not the Gulf of Alaska. Fur seals, bowhead and gray whales are seasonal migrants into the Arctic zone through the Aleutian Islands.

This "Great Land" is the deeply-revered home for Native people who have accepted it on its own terms and successfully adapted their lifestyles to it for more than 500 generations.

Prehistory

Alaska has a special place in human history as the likely route by which the New World came to be occupied. Most archaeologists believe that migration into the New World occurred sometime (perhaps more than once) between 50,000 and 15,000 years ago (ya) during the last ice age. During that time, sea level was as much as 350 feet lower than now.

Petroglyphs, images picked into stones, are found in the coastal regions of the Alutiiq, Tlingit and Haida. (STEPHEN REED CAPPS COLLECTION, ARCHIVES, ALASKA AND POLAR REGIONS DEPARTMENT, UNIVERSITY OF ALASKA-FAIRBANKS)

This linked Siberia and western Alaska into a huge arctic grassland called *Beringia.*

While traditional models of New World settlement have proposed that early people traveled through the central non-coastal area of Beringia (Seward Peninsula to Tanana River), some scholars have more recently suggested the possibility of a southern entry along the Beringian coast, an area that has since been inundated by rising waters of the Bering Sea. No hard evidence presently supports coastal passage as the earliest route into Alaska by maritime peoples but its possibilities continue to intrigue a number of scholars.

An early wave of migrants, called *Paleo-Indians*, probably came into this region in pursuit of mammoth, bison and other large herbivores. They are generally believed to have passed through Alaska, traveling southward to occupy North, Central and South America within several thousand years after first entering the New World. Evidence for the Paleo-Indian tradition in Alaska is limited, brief and found only north of the Yukon River. The Mesa Site, located on the north side of the Brooks Range, is regarded as the earliest evidence of human occupation of Alaska at 11,800 ya. The site, overlooking an enormous landscape in all directions, is located on the flat area on top of the landform. Large chipped projectile points, presumably attached to spears, were manufactured by users of the site as they watched the area below for game.

BLM

This isolated mesa on the north slope of the Brooks Range provided an impressive vista for hunters to watch for game more than 11,800 years ago. It is one of the oldest archaeological sites in Alaska.

Sites in the Tanana River valley have revealed tentative evidence of a seasonal hunting and collecting tradition that used small spear points and arrowheads prior to 11,500 years ago. *Paleo-Arctic* tradition arti-facts, especially *microblades* (small stone hunting tools) and cores similar to those found in certain sites in Siberia have been found at Dry Creek and Broken Mammoth in the Tanana River Valley.

The ancestors of contemporary Alaska Natives are thought to be part of later movements of people into the New World from 10,000-5,000 ya. One hypothesis is that two episodes of immigration occurred, an earlier wave of Indians about 9,000-7,000 ya and a later wave of Eskaleuts about 7,000-6,000 ya. However, there is little agreement about when the earliest migration occurred, how many other migrations occurred or where in Beringia they occurred.

Microblades and cores of the Paleo-arctic tradition have been found in virtually all parts of Alaska except Prince William Sound. No evidence of housing structures has been found with these tools; it is believed that the makers were nomadic hunters and gatherers who pursued a variety of mammals including caribou and bison as well as smaller animals, waterfowl and fish. The distribution of these artifacts indicates people gradually spread throughout Alaska between 11,000 and 7,000 ya. By 2,500 ya, every portion of habitable Alaska had seen some human settlers.

Early Alaskans altered their adaptations after 7,000 ya. Two tendencies are apparent: regional styles of tools and artifacts emerge and the microblade type tools give way to larger projectile points. It has been suggested that this shift parallels a change in the environment in which the boreal forest replaced grasslands in much of Alaska.

About 4,000 ya, the *Arctic Small Tool Tradition* appeared in western Alaska and spread northeastward across the arctic region of Canada to Greenland. Because of its distribution, this tool tradition is considered characteristic of the earliest Eskimo population. Maritime hunting of seals through winter ice emerged and subsequent stages of Eskimo culture developed and refined marine mammal hunting to great sophistication.

After 4,000 ya, the archaeological record becomes much more complicated as innovations in housing types, tools, artistic styles, and burial styles occurred throughout Alaska. The number and size of sites increase indicating an expanding population. Regional variations become relatively distinct and apparently lead to the artifacts and cultural patterns characteristic of Alaska Native groups at the time of contact with Europeans. It must be emphasized, however, that the archaeology of Alaska remains poorly understood and much work remains to be done to reveal the story of Alaskan prehistory.

Discovering the Past

Archeologists investigate questions about previous cultural groups and practices by analyzing the materials people leave behind. *Sites* are the specific locales where *artifacts* (objects clearly modified by humans such as tools, cut bones and pottery) and *features* (structures built by humans such as hearths, house pits and fortifications) remaining from previous human occupancy are found.

When a group of artifacts and features are found at several sites in a given time period, the term *tradition* is used to characterize this pattern. Archeologists are interested not only in tracing the origins and distribution of such traditions (cultural chronology), but are also interested in the distinctive ecological, social and cultural dimensions of traditions. That is, they seek to reconstruct the way of life.

While in some cases the cultural materials observed to be used by Alaska Natives at the time of contact can be identified at sites, the further back in time the materials were deposited, the less reliable it is to link specific materials with specific Alaska Native groups.

Cultural change has been a persistent feature of Alaska Native life during the past 10,000 years. The complexity of the record insures that it will be many years before we clearly understand the complete story of cultural development in Alaska.

72-71-808N

Labrets (plugs inserted through the skin of the lower lip) were commonly worn by Inupiat males and Unangan, Alutiiq, Tlingit and Haida females.
(LOMEN FAMILY COLLECTION, ARCHIVES, ALASKA AND POLAR REGIONS DEPARTMENT, UNIVERSITY OF ALASKA-FAIRBANKS)

Languages

Alaska Native languages fall into two major *language families* (groups of languages which are related). These are the *Eska-Aleutian* and the *Na-Dene*. Languages in the Eska-Aleutian family are separated into Aleut and Eskimo. Eskimo is further subdivided into Inupiaq and Yup'ik groups. The difference between these two languages is roughly the same as between English and other Germanic languages.

The boundary between the two languages groups occurs just north of the mouth of the Yukon River at Unalakleet. From there north on the North American mainland and on Little Diomede Island, forms of Inupiaq are spoken all the way to Greenland in a series of mutually-understandable dialects.

Yup'ik spoken in Alaska is subdivided further into three major mutually-incomprehensible languages:

- Siberian Yup'ik, spoken by the St. Lawrence Island and Siberian Eskimos;
- Central Yup'ik, spoken by a number of groups on the Alaskan mainland from the mouth of the Yukon River south and east to the Alaska Peninsula;
- Alutiiq, spoken along the south side of the Alaskan Peninsula, on Kodiak Island, on the lower part of the Kenai Peninsula and in Prince William Sound.

Languages change when speakers of the same language are isolated from each other. It is estimated that Aleut and the proto-Eskimo language separated 6,000-7,000 ya. Yup'ik and Inupiaq have been separated for about 2,000 years with less time separating the Yup'ik languages.

The Na-Dene language family includes the Athabaskan languages, Eyak, and probably Tlingit. Also included in the Na-Dene family are a number of Athabaskan languages in northern Canada, British Columbia, and California as well as Apache and Navajo of the southwestern United States.

In Alaska, 12 separate Athabaskan languages are recognized. Linguistic evidence suggests Tlingit may have diverged from the other languages as long as 6,000 ya. For the remainder of the Alaskan Athabaskan languages, constant contact among speakers produces a unique situation where distinct languages are recognized yet mutual comprehensibility between speakers is relatively high. Eyak and Tlingit speakers, on the other hand, cannot be understood by speakers of Athabaskan languages. Haida, once thought to be related to Tlingit, is now considered unarelated to any other Alaska language.

Physical characteristics

Alaskan Eskimos are closely related genetically to Siberian peoples such as the Chukchi. In general they are heavy-boned, muscular and lean. They have relatively small hands and relatively short legs in proportion to their height. They are short-to medium in stature with Inupiat populations tending to be considerably taller than Yup'ik populations. Their skin color is quite light and weathers to an olive shade with exposure. They have large heads with relatively flat faces, low-bridged noses, high cheekbones and epicanthic folds in their eyelids. Hair is straight and dark brown to black with little body hair and minimal facial hair among men.

Recent studies indicate that Eskimos have several possible genetic adaptations to cold. Brown *adipose* fat tissue is retained into adulthood in Eskimo populations whereas it is only found in childhood in other human populations. This tissue is metabolized to sustain core body temperatures under cold stress. Hands and feet of Eskimos appear to show greater and more rapid vasoconstriction and dilation than other human populations allowing for greater blood flow, thus maintaining higher temperatures in the hands and feet. Contrary to popular belief, Eskimos do not have more fat than other people.

Alaskan Indians tend to be more closely related genetically to other American Indians than they are to Alaskan Eskimos. Alaskan Indians tend to be medium to tall in stature with long arms, short trunks and long legs. In general, they are angular and moderately built. Skin color is relatively light, darkening to olive or brown with exposure. All have relatively large heads with broad faces but not as broad as Eskimos. Epicanthic folds are occasionally apparent. Hair is straight and coarse from dark brown to black in color; body hair is minimal with moderate amounts of facial hair among males.

Tlingit and Haida tend to be stockier with broad muscular chests and shoulders compared to Athabaskans. Athabaskans tend to have noses with higher bridges while Tlingit and Haida noses tend to be flatter.

Clothing bag made from sealskin

Inupiat in ceremonial costume, Cape Prince of Wales. Drums were made from seal intestine stretched across a circular wooden frame.

(ANCHORAGE MUSEUM OF HISTORY AND ART)

B65.18.774

Unangan baskets, Atka Island, about 1899. Countless hours of work collecting, drying, selecting and weaving grasses transformed mundane household items into artistic marvels. (E. H. HARRIMAN COLLECTION, ARCHIVES, ALASKA AND POLAR REGIONS DEPARTMENT, UNIVERSITY OF ALASKA-FAIRBANKS)

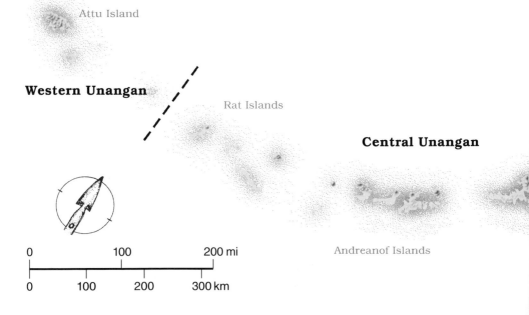

Attu Island

Western Unangan

Rat Islands

Central Unangan

Andreanof Islands

0   100   200 mi

0   100   200   300 km

Unangan artists such as Parascovia Wright practice the delicate art of weaving Attu Island grass baskets.
(Photo by Kathy Kiefer)

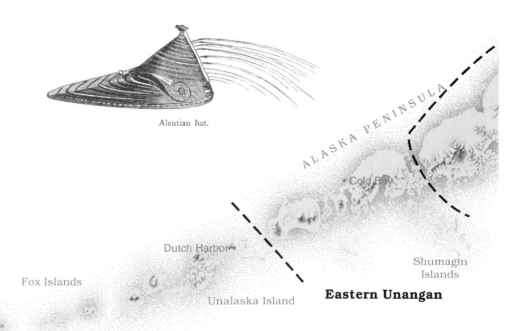

Aleutian hat.

ALASKA PENINSULA

Cold Bay

Fox Islands

Dutch Harbor

Unalaska Island

Shumagin Islands

Eastern Unangan

Unangan/Aleut

CHAPTER 2

Unangan/Aleut

Unangan mask

Stretching like a rocky necklace from Asia to North America, the Aleutian Islands and the nearby Alaska Peninsula are the home of the Unangan, "the original people." The term "Aleut" was introduced by Russians and comes originally from the Koryak or Chukchi languages of Siberia and was adopted by the people to reflect an identity altered by adoption of the Russian Orthodox faith and marriage of Russian men with Unangan women. It appears to have been quickly adopted by the Unangan people themselves (Lantis 1985).

The Unangan are distinctive among the world's people for their remarkably successful maritime adaptation to this cold archipelago. At the time of European contact, the Unangan population inhabited all of the major Aleutian Islands, the Alaska Peninsula as far east as Port Moller, and the Shumagin Islands to the south of the Alaska Peninsula.

Archaeology

William Laughlin, an early archaeologist in the Aleutian Islands, considered the Unangan the survivors of the inundation of the Bering land bridge at the end of the Ice Age 10,000 ya (years ago). His work at Anangula, a site on Umnak Island in the central Aleutians, demonstrated that people lived there as early as 8,500 ya. The microblades and cores found at the oldest levels of Anangula are similar to Paleo-Arctic tradition artifacts found in interior Alaska several thousand years earlier. Post holes indicate that several shelters or simple houses were located at the site; proximity to the ocean indicates that people were dependent on marine resources but no materials have survived to confirm this.

Between 6,000 and 4,000 ya, several sites indicate the expansion of populations onto other islands in the central Aleutian Archipelago. Continuous occupation at Chaluka, a site surrounded by the contemporary village of Nikolski, from 4,000 ya demonstrates the continuity of the Unangan people. Fish hooks, barbed projectile points, harpoon heads, and other objects remain constant in the archaeological record until the time of contact indicating the maritime focus of life.

Around 3,000 ya, Unangan or their ancestors appear to have built several multi-household communities on the rich lagoons at the west end of the Alaska Peninsula. Large houses with whale bone frames have been found as far east as Port Moller during this time period. At the same time, groups were also moving into the Shumagin Islands. Artifacts considered to be used by bearers of the Arctic Small Tool Tradition, already found further up the Alaska Peninsula at Ugashik Narrows and Naknek, have been found near the west end of the Alaska Peninsula. This finding sets up the possibility of close contact between groups, at least for a short period of time.

Unangan expanded to the west somewhat later, arriving at their furthermost outposts on Attu Island about 1,500 ya.

Population and Settlement

Although reconstruction of Unangan culture and history is difficult due to the devastating impact of Russian contact in the 18th century, it is believed that the Unangan were divided into nine named subdivisions. The total Unangan population is estimated to have been between 15,000-18,000 people at the time of contact. The nine subdivisions are usually divided into western, central and eastern groups based on

"Oulak, Chief Village on Unalaska" **by Louis Choris, ca 1825. The treeless, windswept Aleutian Islands were first colonized by the Unangan more than 8,000 years ago. The steep, rocky shores made the occasional flat terrance immediately above a sandy beach, a valuable site.** (ANCHORAGE MUSEUM OF HISTORY AND ART)

language. Population concentration was greatest among the eastern groups who had access to salmon and caribou. The Unangan were a relatively long-lived people with a considerable portion of the populaton more than 60 years of age.Unangan settlements included villages and seasonal camps. Winter villages, which could be used year round, were generally placed in protected locations along a shoreline with a good beach, a nearby freshwater stream, a headland for observation, and close proximity to marine mammals, fish and intertidal resources. On the mainland, settlements tended to be on the southside of the Alaska Peninsula, perhaps to avoid winter ice from the Bering Sea. In the Aleutian Islands, settlements often were located on the north side, probably to avoid the prevailing southwest winds. A typical village consisted of about 200 people living in five-to ten dwellings. Tents or abandoned houses were used at seasonal camps where people gathered food.

Houses

The basic house of the Unangan is called a *barabara* (a Siberian term). Barabaras were oblong pit dwellings with wooden or whale bone frames and rafters overlain by grass and sod. Often they were nearly indistinguishable from the surrounding terrain. Barabaras were normally entered by means of a pole ladder through an entryway in the ceiling. Their typical dimensions were 35-to 40 feet long by 20-to 30 feet

20868

The traditional Unangan house, the barabara, was a sod-covered dugout typically entered through a hole in the roof. This barabara's door indicates Russian influence. (HEALY COLLECTION, HENRY E. HUNTINGTON LIBRARY)

wide with the floor being four-to six feet below ground level. The inside consisted of an open space in the middle portion for general living and compartmentalized, three-foot deep trenches along the walls for sleeping. These were separated by grass mats hung from the rafters. Sometimes compartments were dug into the earthwalls for burials.

Tools, baskets and other objects were manufactured in the open area. A trough of urine was kept there. Uric acid was used by most Alaskan Native groups for purposes like washing hair (a freshwater rinse would be used afterward), softening skins or making dyes.

The Unangan heated their houses with oil lamps and occasionally small hearths. They usually cooked outside the home near storage and refuse pits. Apparently there were no large community houses or steambaths in Unangan villages. However, some extremely large houses, evidently occupied by several families, have recently been discovered in the eastern area.

Food and diet

The most important animal to the Unangan was the Steller sea lion. This animal provided not only food but also a vast variety of other products including boat covers (hide), line and cord (sinew), oil (blubber), tools (bones), fishhooks (teeth), boot soles (flippers), containers (stomach) and materials for garments (esophagus and intestines). Other important marine mammals were seals, sea otters and whales which together with the sea lion comprised 50 percent of the diet. Bottomfish such as halibut and cod comprised about one-third of the diet.

Unangan whaling was a highly ritualized activity for which men and their wives prepared themselves by abstinence and other behaviors to make themselves worthy. Men hunted whales alone with harpoons from kayaks. The stone harpoon heads were coated with a "magical" poison concocted from the aconite plant. Once wounded, the whale could live several days to a week as the poison slowly worked. During this time the hunter who struck the whale secluded himself in his house and pretended to be ill hoping that the whale likewise would become sick and die. Other hunters would watch the whale to see what happened. If the whale died nearby, it was towed to the beach. Whales wounded but lost were often recovered by other Aleuts when they washed ashore.

Not all Unangan engaged in whaling. In the eastern areas, Unangan hunted caribou and fished for salmon. Unangan fishermen caught halibut and cod with ingenious wooden hooks and line made of braided kelp or sea lion sinew.

Women, children and the elderly concentrated on collecting bird eggs, intertidal organisms (such as chitons, clams, seas urchins and seaweed) and plants, roots and berries which ripened in the late summer and fall.

81.68.4

(above) "Inhabitants of the Aleutian Islands," **hand-colored lithograph done about 1825 by Louis Choris (1795-1828). The distinctive Unangan visors were made from wood and had sea lion whiskers for decoration. The visors shielded a hunter's face from sun and rain.**

(right) **Unangan dancing masks have been found in burials in the Shumagin and Aleutian islands. Note the holes on the edges to attach the mask to the head.** (BOTH FROM ANCHORAGE MUSEUM OF HISTORY AND ART.)

B81.64.1

Technology and training

Unangan are world famous for their unparalleled skill in handling the *baidarka* (or kayak, Unangan—*chigak*), the distinctive skin boat they mastered. Males trained from an early age in the skills necessary to hunt, handle watercraft and survive in the rough waters around the Aleutian Islands. These craft were outfitted ingeniously with throwing boards and a variety of darts for different species attached to the deck within immediate reach of the hunter. Inside the craft were ballast to keep it upright, a bailer, a float and a sewing kit to fix tears on the fly. Unangan men used centuries of accumulated knowledge of wind, tide and current to successfully travel not only throughout the islands but far beyond up into Bristol Bay and along the Alaska Peninsula to the Kodiak Archipelago. Unangan also used the *baidar*, a large open skin boat, for travel and trade.

The training of an Unangan male from his youth included the systematic stretching of leg and shoulder muscles. This enabled him to endure the long hours of concentration and stillness necessary if the arduous and time-consuming pursuit of seals and sea otter was to be successful. The boy's shoulder muscles had to be strengthened to achieve maximum velocity and accuracy with the throwing board (or *atlatl*) which was used to cast darts and harpoons at birds and marine mammals.

Despite the cultural emphasis on male hardiness and self-reliance, there was a recognized role in Unangan society for the male transvestite (or *berdache*) who dressed and worked as a woman. They were often considered experts in healing.

Unangan women were trained from early childhood in the important sewing, weaving and food processing skills. In later life this training would insure that their husbands were appropriately outfitted for hunting. Aleut basketry made from the fine grasses of the islands as well as from the spruce roots is some of the finest in the world.

Clothing and decoration

Unangan women constructed marvelous waterproof *kamleikas* (men's outer garments) by painstakingly stitching together strips of sea lion intestine. Waterproof boots were made from sea otter flippers. Colorful cloaks for ceremonial occasions were crafted from the skins of hundreds of tufted puffins taken with snares. Women commonly wore luxurious capes and garments of sea otter fur.

Distinctive elements of Unangan clothing were the beautiful visors and elongate hats worn by the men. Functional designs worn for daily use kept the incessant rain off the hunter and protected his eyes from the ocean's glare. Elegant ceremonial hats were painted in striped curving designs of different colors, often with sea lion whiskers attached for additional decoration.

Supplementary personal adornment existed for both men and women. Simple tattoos, usually from short straight lines, were inscribed on the hands and faces. Nose pins were worn by men and women. *Labrets* (flat circular discs made of wood or ivory) were inserted into slits in the area between the lower lip and the chin. A common style was to wear one below each corner of the mouth. The labret is an extremely old adornment, appearing more than 4,000 years ago in the Unangan cultural record. It is no longer worn. (See page 10.)

Social organization

Matrilineal (traced through the female) descent and inheritance characterized Aleut kinship patterns. Although a house was owned by a woman, usually her brothers and their wives were the primary occupants. A recognized leader of the house, usually the eldest male, made most decisions for the group. Children, particularly males, lived

Russian Orthodox church, Atka, Alaska. Russian Orthodox clerics tried to stop many abuses against the Unangan. Russian Orthodoxy is still a major religion among the Unangan today. (PHOTO BY DOUGLAS VELTRE)

with their mothers during infancy but moved in mid-childhood to the home of their mother's brother. This practice, termed the *avunculate*, makes the uncle the primary teacher and trainer of his sister's children. The uncle's role was generally a strict one in order to insure the competence of the young man. The boy's father assumed a sympathetic, reassuring and supportive role.

Most marriages were monogamous although *polygyny* (multiple wives) occurred among wealthier, more powerful leaders. Divorce was possible, although rare in Unangan society; when desired, a woman simply returned to her own home or that of her eldest sister.

There is little evidence of more complex social organization among the Unangan beyond the house group. There were no men's houses and probably no clans. Although each house group was apparently independent, a senior or leading house in a community was recognized and its head was considered the village leader. The Russians introduced the term *toyon* for this person. Coordination of movement to camps by several house groups and even the village occurred periodically since villages were composed of closely-related people. The village leader was primarily responsible for decisions concerning war and peace.

Unangan society was roughly divided into three classes—wealthy people, common people, and slaves (Lantis 1984). The wealthy and common people were usually closely related, thus minimizing conflict. Only whale hunting and possibly leadership were inherited. The number of slaves, primarily women, is thought to have been small.

Warfare

Although there were no formal village boundaries, Unangan communities claimed certain areas as their resource territories such as rookeries, fishing banks and beaches. These areas would be closely watched. Other Unangan using those areas were considered trespassers if they had not requested access. Normally, however, people would simply go to the nearest village where customs of generosity would ensure that they would be well fed. Poachers could be evicted or attacked.

Warfare was not uncommon among the Unangan. Accounts tell of battles waged over long distances with the Koniag people of Kodiak Island, the Eskimo groups of the Alaska Peninsula and even the Chugach in Prince William Sound. Slat armor constructed of tightly-woven wooden rods have been found; however, Unangan legends state that only the heads of a household wore armor (Laughlin 1980). Hostilities often took the form of raids in which small groups of men, usually less than 10, attacked another village to avenge some insult or theft or to obtain women as slaves. Men who participated did so generally by choice rather than by order.

Aleutian Island Mummies

The special importance of death and the spirit of the deceased is apparent in the distinctive mummification practices of the Unangan. On Kagamil Island, an amazing 234 excellently-preserved bodies have been discovered in several caves. According to William Laughlin, a widely-recognized expert on the Aleuts, mummification was practiced to preserve the spiritual power which resides in each person. These powers could be solicited at a later time by emboldened Unangan hunters who visited the caves and took a bit of flesh from one of the mummies, hoping it would bring assistance in whaling. But this was dangerous and those who sought such power might be subject to insanity, severe sickness, and early death. Even the kin of whalers who sought the power of the mummies could suffer harm from the spirit forces unleashed.

Scientific studies have revealed a detailed Unangan understanding of human anatomy. Mummification is dependent on two factors: deactivating tissue-destroying enzymes in the body and halting invasion of the body by microorganisms that decompose the flesh and soft tissue. Both are best accomplished by warmth and dryness as found in the arid regions of Egypt and Chile. The Unangan controlled these processes by extracting the viscera from the body, inserting dry grass into the cavity and constantly drying the body for up to a month after death. The body was kept in a flexed position bent at the knees. Prior to entombment, the body was wrapped first with multiple layers of seal or sea lion intestine, then with clothing and finally with skins or mats. Often it was placed in a wooden cradle or upon a raised platform in the cave.

The final secret to Unangan mummification was their choice of warm, dry caves for placing the bodies. The Aleutian Islands are noted for their volcanic activity. Subsurface heat escaping through cracks to the surface in the chosen caves insured that the mummies had optimal conditions for preservation. Burial caves with these characteristics have been found in several locations. Although the practice of mummification is ancient and continued even after early contact with Europeans, it has now been abandoned.

Ceremonies

Good relationships were maintained between communities through winter festivities of dancing and feasting. The village chief from one village would invite another village to visit. The visitors would arrive in their best clothing and were housed and fed generously by their hosts. After changing into ceremonial costume, dancers with tambourine drums from each group took turns trying to outperform each other. Women danced while shaking rattles made of inflated bladders. Wooden masks were used in some dances to invoke the presence of powerful spirits. Distinctive wooden masks with exceptionally large, broad noses and a slightly wolf-like appearance have been found in burials in different parts of Unangan territory. Wrestling and storytelling were also favorite entertainments with exceptional performers given respect and honored status.

Occasions of special significance and ceremony in the Unangan life cycle were marriage, puberty and especially death. Following most deaths, viscera were removed and the body cavity stuffed with grass. Then the person would be propped up in the corner of the house on a mat specially woven for them or placed in wooden cradle-like frame suspended over the normal sleeping place. There the corpse would remain for as long as several months. People felt no horror of the dead but rather a deep sense of loss and wished to prolong the presence of the deceased. Most of the dead were then buried in the house walls or under the floor. Another form of burial, *mummification*, was unique among the Unangan. It was apparently practiced only in the eastern and central areas and is associated with whaling specialists.

Beliefs

Although little is known of the Unangan belief system, they appear to have conceived of a creator deity related to the sun who was instrumental in hunting success and the reincarnation of souls. Small images of the creator, known as *kaathaagaathagh*, were carved from ivory and hung from the ceiling beams (Laughlin 1980). The creator, however, had little impact on everyday life which was instead influenced by two classes of spirits, good and evil. Animals also had spirits. The most important ones were those of the whale and sea otter. Aleut men wore a variety of amulets and charms that were thought to provide special powers from the animal spirits to enhance success in hunting. The Unangan believed in the reincarnation of souls which migrated between the earth, a world below and a world above.

Behavior patterns

Unangan life was laid out in a clear and dignified manner. Appropriate behaviors were taught and reinforced from early childhood. An Unangan did not speak unless something important needed to be said. Men kept silent lookout vigils for hours on end, then retired without saying a word to anyone. If animosity developed, men duelled verbally. Each man had to listen to his antagonist without showing anger. When near the end of life, some Unangan men went out in their kayaks never to return. Women tirelessly worked on clothing and baskets for hours at a time. All respected the actions of others and were careful not to offend or insult. Positive reinforcement rather than punishment maintained harmony in Unangan communities. In the 18th century, a violent group of men, driven by the ruthless quest for profits at any cost, descended on the Unangan, and their coming eventually resulted in the destruction of this unique system of cultural adaptations.

Contact and experience with Europeans

In 1741, the Danish explorer Vitus Bering, in the employ of the Russian government, made the first European landing in Alaska. The discovery of millions of sea otter quickly prompted commercial efforts by independent fur trappers and traders of Cossack descent known as *promyshlenniki*. They sought furs and used a variety of techniques from trade to theft to their ultimate technique, taking wives hostage, in order to coerce Unangan men into hunting for them. The Unangan fought back and were able to inflict several defeats on the invaders. By the late 1780s, however, effective Unangan resistance had been broken and the Russians subjugated them. The tremendous skill of the Unangan men as open-ocean hunters was irreplaceable. They were quickly incorporated as the backbone of the Russian-American Company, a monopoly authorized by the Czar in 1790 to control activities in Alaska. Unangan men were taken from their ancestral homes as far as the Santa Catalina Islands off southern California and forced to hunt sea otters and fur seals for the Russians.

In 1786, the Russians discovered the Pribilof Islands. The two main islands, Saint Paul and Saint George, are the major fur seal breeding grounds in the North Pacific. The Russians forcibly relocated a group of Aleut to harvest the seals; descendants of those first Unangan continue to occupy the Pribilof Islands to this day.

The combination of warfare, disease and starvation wiped out entire villages, reducing the Unangan people to less then 20 percent of the precontact level. In the 19th century, the Russian government tightened control over the commercial activities of the Russian-American Company and sent Russian Orthodox priests to Alaska. Although they established hospitals, schools, and created an Unangan *orthography* (writing system), it was far too little too late for the devastated Unangan to recover.

The Unangan of Unalaska built massive semi-subterranean houses just prior to Russian discovery. Some were more than 100 feet long and 50 feet wide, consisting of a central room and six-to ten side rooms. In this photo of an excavated house, white cylinders mark the rocks that were placed under the posts that framed the central room. These large structures imply greater coordination, leadership and class differences, possibly resulting from increased warfare. (PHOTO BY DOUGLAS VELTRE.)

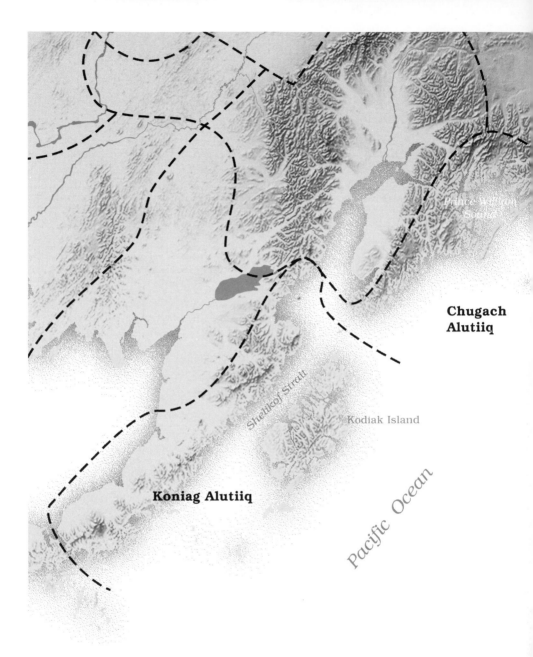

**Chugach
Alutiiq**

*Prince William
Sound*

Shelikof Strait

Kodiak Island

Pacific Ocean

Koniag Alutiiq

**Natives paddling near Port Dick in
Cook Inlet. From an engraving by
Harry Humphries made in 1798.**
(ANCHORAGE MUSEUM OF HISTORY AND ART)

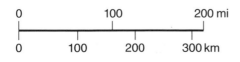

| 0 | | 100 | | 200 mi |

| 0 | 100 | 200 | 300 km |

Eyak

Sugpiaq/Alutiiq

Pacific Eskimos

CHAPTER 3

Sugpiaq/Alutiiq

Pacific Eskimos

B86.94.10.46

B86.94.10.47

Chugach Alutiiq men and women were dramatically adorned for various occasions. The man's spruce root hat suggests contact between the Chugach and Tlingit who wore similar hats. (ENGRAVING BY J. WEBBER, 1780. ANCHORAGE MUSEUM OF HISTORY AND ART)

The coastal arc of the Gulf of Alaska from the southwest end of Kodiak Island to the Copper River delta might be visualized as a gigantic teeter-totter. Lands dip and rise along the tectonic interface where the Pacific Plate collides and descends beneath the North American Plate. This dynamic and dangerous zone of steep coastal mountains, earthquakes and volcanic eruptions is characterized by a grassy Aleutian-type ecosystem along the Alaska Peninsula and the western part of the Kodiak Archipelago and forested Sitkan-type ecosystem from the northeastern Kodiak Archipelago through the lower Kenai Peninsula to Prince William Sound. In this region are the only heavily-forested environments along the entire sweep from Siberia to Greenland in which bearers of "Eskimo" cultural characteristics developed long-term adaptations. The Kodiak Archipelago has limited terrestrial resources being home only to the exceptionally large brown bears and to foxes, making marine and riverine resources vital to the people livng there.

Sugpiaq-speaking people of the Yup'ik language group occupy this region. While the term Sugpiaq is the older term of self-identification, Alutiiq came into usage around 1980 in response to linguistic studies and a desire of speakers to distinguish themselves from their Central Yup'ik neighbors across the Alaska Peninsula. Most Kodiak Archipelago, Alaska and Kenai Peninsula and Prince William Sound people came to self-identify as Aleut after subjugation by Russian invaders. The term "Alutiiq" was crafted using Sugpiaq word formation principles from the word "Aleut" and will be used in the remainder of this discussion to designate the peoples of this region.

These groups have sometimes been referred to as Pacific Eskimo by anthropologists based on the fact the Alutiiq language is closely related to Central Yup'ik and not to Unangan/Aleut. This characterization, however, is not popular with the Alutiiq people themselves. Linguists have estimated that Alutiiq and Central Yup'ik have been separated as languages for less than 1,000 years.

Three basic subdivisions of the Alutiiq are recognized. The Koniagmiut (now also referred to as Qikertarmiut) occupied the Kodiak Archipelago and primarily the south side of the Alaska Peninsula, the Chugachmiut occupied Prince William Sound, and the Unergkurmiut lived along the south coast of the Kenai Peninsula and along Kachemak Bay.

Koniagmiut and Chugachmiut spoke distinct dialects of the Alutiiq language but communicated easily with one another. The terms Koniag and Chugach will be used in the remainder of this chapter to refer to these regional subdivisions.

Archaeology

The Alutiiq region is one of Alaska's great ancestral interaction zones. The people of the region were both initiators and recipients of cultural influences that were shared with other Alaskan groups. Initial settlement of the Kodiak Archipelago and Alaska Peninsula immediately opposite took place slightly before 7,500 ya (years ago) by Paleo-Arctic microblade-bearing people. By 7,300 ya, Kodiak Island's new residents

This remarkable wooden carving of an apparently-pregnant female was discovered during archaeological excavations at Karluk. The placement of the hands on the lower back suggests the piece may have been used to inform young women on procedures for assisting in childbirth. (ALUTIIQ MUSEUM/ ARTIFACT OWNED BY KONIAG, INC.)

exhibited distinctive elements of a new tradition termed *Ocean Bay*. The implements designed by these peoples include perhaps the first oil lamps and large semi-lunar knives (known later as *ulus*). In addition, long (up to 20-inch) slate blades, barbed bone and antler harpoon heads used for harvesting large sea mammals also proliferate. Steller sea lion, migratory whales (minke, humpback, sperm and gray), harbor seals, and sea otters apparently became the food focus of these early peoples. The Ocean Bay tradition is considered one of the ancient sources of sea mammal hunting in the north Pacific Ocean region.

Some people utilizing Ocean Bay technologies apparently migrated to the northeast, settling in Kachemak Bay on the lower Kenai Peninsula by around 5,000 ya.

This extraordinary lamp from Uyak Bay would have been a stunning vision when filled with oil. The animal's head would have appeared to be rising from the ocean. The exquisite quality and rarity of such lamps suggest they may have been used only in rituals.

Beginning around 3,800 ya, major changes appear to have occurred in the Kodiak Archipelago. A new tradition, known as *Kachemak* (based on the name of the bay where it was first identified in the 1930s), is distinguished from its predecessor by among other things, an abundance of notched cylindrical stones. These stones are considered evidence for using weighted nets for fishing, primarily for salmon and herring, and became a major focus of subsistence activity at this time. Hooks for taking halibut and cod from the ocean bottom are abundant in Kachemak sites. Kachemak people maintained sea mammal hunting and utilization. The beautiful and symbolically rich oil lamps produced during this time illustrate how important marine mammals were to the Kachemak people.

The Kachemak tradition also is characterized by elaborate and distinctive burial practices involving body dismemberment. Labrets, beads and other items of adornment appear in different sizes and materials with certain burials containing larger and greater numbers of these items. This variability in grave goods indicates that Kachemak people likely practiced status differentiation and social hierarchy.

Kachemak people expanded northward out of Kachemak Bay up the Kenai Peninsula, perhaps even for a short period of time into the Susitna River valley.

The Gulf of Alaska-fronting coast of the Kenai Peninsula has seen little archaeological investigation and, at present, the earliest occupation is dated to about 1,750 ya.

How long people lived in Prince William Sound is not as clear as elsewhere in the Alutiiq region, but we think it began about 4,000-3,500 ya. Marine mammal hunting was likely the central focus of Prince William Sound people but in a less-abundant ecosystem than the Kodiak Archipelago provided.

Beginning around 2,000 ya, an important environmental shift is evident as the characteristic flora of the temperate rainforest to the southeast began to gradually spread across the central Gulf of Alaska region. The coniferous forest dominated by Sitka spruce appeared in Prince William Sound about 2,000 ya and in the northeastern Kodiak Archipelago about 1,100 ya. The appearance of adzes and other wood-working tools demonstrate that resident ancestral Alutiiq began to incorporate wood into their technological repertoires. Spruce root hats, baskets, wooden vessels and containers and other wood products likely date from this period.

Between 1,000 and 600 ya, another shift in artifacts and cultural practices appears to have occurred parts of the Alutiiq region. One of the major developments of this time is the disappearance of riverine Kachemak peoples from the central Kenai Peninsula. The appearance of sweat baths, ceramics in the western part of the region, incised pebbles, large, multi-room houses and perhaps wood slat armor are considered markers of the new tradition, *Koniag*. This tradition is considered to be the basis of the cultural systems operating among most Alutiiq peoples at the time of historic contact. In the discussion of cultural traits that follows, Koniag and Chugach variations on the Alutiiq pattern will be noted where they occur.

Population and settlement pattern

Estimates of the size and density of Alutiiq populations at contact vary considerably. Based on Russian sources, the pre-contact population of the Kodiak Archipelago has been estimated at approximately 8,000 people. Recent archaeological research, however, has revealed very large sites along salmon systems leading some scholars to revise their estimates upward to 12-15,000 residents of the Kodiak Archipelago alone. The Alaska Peninsula by contrast was probably occupied by less than 1,000 people and the outer Kenai Peninsula by less than 500 people.

Population figures for the Chugach range widely as well. At the lower

Alutiiq Groups and Estimated Population at Contact	
Alaska Peninsula	1,000
Lower Kenai Peninsula	500
Kodiak Archipelago	12,000 to 15,000
Prince William Sound	1,500 to 2,000

end are estimates of 800 and at the upper end estimates of 3500. The small size and wide distribution of sites in Prince William Sound have puzzled scholars who now think the Chugach numbered between 1,500 and 2,000 at contact.

The Koniagmiut and Chugachmiut were both divided into approximately eight local sociopolitical groups. These can be considered territorially-based units as they protected their territories against unwanted outside incursions and respected the territories of their neighbors. There were at least 65 communities located in the Kodiak Archipelago, perhaps 10 along the Alaska Peninsula and another 10-12 in Prince William Sound.

Settlement patterns in the Alutiiq area include consolidated winter villages as well as numerous spring, summer and fall seasonal encampments. In the Kodiak Archipelago, a major dimension in community size and subsistence orientation is the abundance of salmon runs. Where there are large sockeye salmon systems, fishing was a central focus of activity while in other areas, marine mammal hunting was more important. One of the largest Alaska Native communities (or sets of communities) at contact was the lagoon at the mouth of the Karluk River, second only in Alaska to the Kvichak River draining Lake Iliamna as a source of sockeye salmon. No less than 800 people occupied the lagoon with probably an additional 1,000 people living along the course of the river to Karluk Lake. The continuity of these communities for more than 500 years, depending throughout on salmon, suggests the development of sustainable fishing practices that maintained the resource.

Other than in the vicinity of the largest salmon streams, Koniag communities were small and dispersed. Winter villages, in protected locations and near good areas for winter cod and halibut fishing, ranged from 100-200 residents in five-to 10 houses.

Chugach communities generally fell in the 100-200 person range. These were generally located in areas with nearby access to winter bottom fishing and sea mammal hunting but salmon were also important.

Koniag and Chugach communities also had *refuge areas*. These were hidden retreats such as caves or islands with steep cliffs where people could go in times of danger or attack.

Housing and facilities

Buildings in the Alutiiq area consist of two basic designs—the house and the community center (or *kazhim* as the Russians labeled it). Among the Koniag, the house *(ciqullaq)* was partially subterranean with either a surface doorway or in a few cases a tunnel entryway. According to Russian figures, approximately 20 people resided in such a house. The basic floor plan consisted of four partially-buried wooden posts laid out

The semi-subterranean homes of the Alutiiq combined wood, grass and sod materials and were called barabaras by the Russians. (AMY STEFFIAN)

in a square or rectangle buried in the floor about 10-12 feet apart but house sizes varied substantially. Inter-notched beams were cribbed upward to form the roof. Planks were laid on the along the side of the cribbing and across the roof, then covered with grass and sod. An opening serving as skylight and smoke hole was left in the middle of the roof that would be covered with a translucent piece of animal intestine.

Inside there was a central open area with a hearth in the center. This was primarily a women's work area as well as the cooking area. Some Koniag houses had storage pits near the walls that were covered with stone slabs.

Along the sides of the house, smaller rooms carved out of the earth were used for sleeping. Some side rooms had earthen platforms covered with planks while others had planks inserted into the wall to form a ledge for sleeping. Small entryways connected these side rooms to the main room. At the opposite end of the house away from the entrance was the room typically occupied by the head couple of the household.

Most Koniag houses had at least one side room that served as a steam bath. These rooms can be identified archaeologically by the substantial quantities of fire-cracked rock found buried in the walls or packed into the corners of the room. Steaming provided a combination of cleansing, spiritual purification, relaxation and socializing for the people.

Outside the Koniag house were a variety of pits and racks. The pits were used for food storage, cooking, and refuse. Along the Karluk River, several Koniag households had clay-lined pits outside the houses. This innovation likely assisted in the retention of oil from sea mammal blubber and preventing non-human uses of the food.

The other basic building found in Koniag communities was the kazhim or community house. This structure was built by a group of families, usually headed by male relatives, and served as the men's work and meeting area during the day. They were larger than normal houses as the four corner posts were positioned 20-25 feet apart in a near square design. Benches were built into the walls for sitting and storage. Men's implements and tools were manufactured and maintained here. According to Russian sources, kazhims were used as assembly halls on certain occasions when the entire community would gather to discuss events that would affect everyone. Finally, the kazhim became the ceremonial structure during the winter festivities, religious rituals and ceremonies.

The kazhim was apparently not a general feature of Chugach life but may have been utilized by one or two groups.

Subsistence: technologies and practices

Stone tools were fundamental in the making of various implements. Various flints and cherts were chipped or ground into sharpened edges to make ulus for cutting skins, making sinew out of whale muscle, scraping and cleaning skins, and numerous other uses. A wide range of materials was used for other tools including bone, antler, shell, ivory and wood. Bone and antler were commonly used for fishhooks and barbed harpoon heads. Shell was used for small sharpened points and ivory appeared as beads and pendants in various adornments. Wood was commonly used in the Prince William Sound, lower Kenai Peninsula and northeastern Kodiak Archipelago areas for containers, headgear and, of course, everywhere as framing material for boats.

The Alutiiq cultural pattern is based on the ability to successfully function in the cold but ice-free waters of the north Pacific Ocean. There can be no doubt about their success in this regard as the Koniag traveled to isolated Chirikof Island and established a community and the Chugach traveled to and from Middleton Island, a lonely spot of land more than thirty miles south of Prince William Sound in the Gulf of Alaska. Among the Koniag, the wood-frame, skin-covered baidarka was most commonly of the two-holed variety, however both single and triple-holed varieties were also used. This meant that the primary marine mammal and ocean fishing productive unit consisted of two males, more than likely related. Among the Chugach the three-holed variety apparently became most common following the arrival of the Russians.

In addition to the baidarkas, the Alutiiq built and used larger open boats consisting of frames covered by skins, usually of sea lion, carefully

28.33

At this Chugach camp in Prince William Sound, the use of wood is apparent in the shelters erected on shore. The baidarka and upside-down baidars show the Chugach used the same type of water transportation as their Koniag relatives.
(Alaska and Polar Regions Collection, University of Alaska-Fairbanks)

stitched together. These could be up to 20 feet in length and were used to transport families or groups of men on visiting, trading or war activities.

When in their baidarkas, Alutiiq men wore a translucent, water-repellant *kamleika*. Alutiiq women sewed a slender strand of grass along the stitch line joining two strips that would absorb moisture and expand thus improving the waterproof quality of the garment.

Alutiiq men wore two primary varieties of headgear at sea, a circular, spruce root hat and a bentwood visor. A very elaborate type of visored headgear was worn by the Koniag whalers that was a symbolic component of their ritualized hunting transformation into a type of killer whale.

Alutiiq men hunted with the throwing board for sea otters, harbor seals, sea lions and whales. In Prince William Sound the Chugach also hunted porpoise. The hunter sat in the bow while his partner in the stern did the paddling and orienting.

The most elaborate and ritualized food-procuring practice among the Alutiiq was whale hunting. Whalers were ritual and knowledge specialists who were viewed with both awe and horror by their fellow Alutiiq.

Alutiiq whaling was designed to take advantage of the convoluted shoreline of both the Kodiak Archipelago and Prince William Sound. Koniag whalers left their villages and went to solitary retreats in caves or secluded coves in April, perhaps a month prior to the arrival of whales, to ritually transform themselves. Whalers had special symbols, such as stars and crabs, and colors painted on their baidarkas and paddles. They had to activate their amulets or talismans through ritual procedures to access their power. Some may have applied aconite poisoning to the tip of their whale harpoon heads.

Perhaps the most unique practice of the Koniag whaler was the use of rendered human fat in their hunting. Whalers exhumed the bodies of recently buried persons—former whalers or persons of high status were preferred—carved off the fleshy, fatty portions of the body and boiled them. It was believed that whales were repulsed by human fat and would not come near it. When a whale was found inside a bay, the whaler would go to the narrowest area at the entrance and pour a line of fat across the entrance. Then he would proceed into the bay and after vocally calling on his spiritual supporters and the sun for assistance, would go and harpoon the whale. Once the whale was struck, the whaler would use song and motion to "tow" the whale ashore. Throughout these preparations and practices, the whaler's wife, who had remained behind in the village, had a strict set of behaviors she was to follow including not leaving the house, limiting her movements and keeping her voice down. Once the whale died and was beached, other village residents would come to cut it up and transport the portions back to the village.

At the conclusion of the whaling season, the whaler had to ritually cleanse and "decommission" himself. Only by transforming himself back to his other human form would he be able to return to the village and live.

Among the Chugach, whaling was conducted in a related but different fashion. Whalers had to go through a similar set of ritual preparations and also were said to use human fat to keep struck whales in the bays. Chugach whaling may have occasionally involved more than one whaler and actual towing of the whale ashore may have been practiced. In both areas, it appears that whaling was an inherited activity, passed from father to son. The mummified burials found in the Kodiak Archipelago and in Prince William Sound are thought to have been whalers.

In addition to sea mammal hunting, salmon fishing, and bottom fishing, Koniag and Chugach subsistence included collecting shellfish and other intertidal organisms, harvesting greens, and collecting large quantities of berries in the fall.

Material culture: objects and adornment

Alutiiq material culture was rich and varied. A variety of objects were created to meet varied needs and objectives characteristic of the Alutiiq cultural system. Various kinds of rock art are found in the Koniag, lower Cook Inlet, and Chugach regions. *Petroglyphs*, created by engraving a design in rock, are found at various locations in the Kodiak archipelago. Rock paintings made by the application of ochre-based pigments to flat stone surfaces are found in lower Cook Inlet and in Prince William Sound. The Chugach paintings in Prince William Sound are believed to be ritual art forms made by whalers to call up powerful spiritual assistance for their hunting efforts.

Archaeological excavations at sites in the Karluk Lagoon region have recovered a rich array of wood and stone objects. Some of the smaller objects include bear's heads and an extraordinary figurine that depicts a human to bird transformation. Carved wooden figures demonstrating excellent representational artistry of males and females, usually four-to eight inches long, are another type of object.

Another type of figure is the shaman's doll. Each village was reputed to have one. It was used by the shaman only during the winter masked ceremonies. Prior to the beginning of the masked ceremonies, the shaman brought out the doll and visited each household where the heads placed markers on the doll indicating what they hoped the spirits would provide for them during the upcoming season.

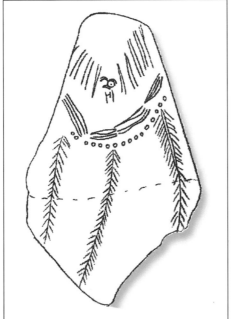

One of the most distinctive types of objects found are flat slate stones with pecked designs into them known now as "talking rocks". The rocks discovered at Karluk depict humans, basically the upper two-thirds of the body, with various types of clothing, jewelry and head-gear.

Incised pebble (circa 1300-1550 AD) excavated from the Settlement Point Site during Dig Afognak. (Artifact owned by Afognak Native Corporation. Drawing by Brian Davis)

Personal adornment took various forms among the Alutiiq. Men and women had different styles of ceremonial clothing and headgear. Male clothing was of sea mammal skins and female clothing was of bird skins. The basic garment was a long, hoodless tunic-style robe that could be made from a variety of materials or dressed up with various designs and embellishments. Labrets were of different size, styles and materials with ivory and jet stone being among the most valuable. In addition, ceremonial self-presentation included septal pins, earrings, and necklaces. Some men and women also had relatively limited tattoos, usually single lines encircling the face or crossing the cheeks. Facial painting was used by both the Koniag and Chugach with black and red being the primary colors. Among the Koniag these were utilized by shamans and others who participated in ritual ceremonies. Chugach appear to have utilized facial painting on more occasions.

At dances and feasts, young girls wore elegant, beaded headdresses with long trailers cascading down their backs that demonstrated elite social position. Prior to contact, dentalium (slender white shells from Vancouver Island obtained in trade) was the preferred material to indicate elevated status here and elsewhere in Alaska. (COURTESY OF ARCTIC STUDIES CENTER, NATIONAL MUSEUM OF NATURAL HISTORY)

Social organization

Kinship practices, such as descent and marriage patterns, indicate that Koniag and Chugach were likely matrilineal and that inheritance followed lineage lines. Women owned the houses. Monogamy was standard but both polygyny (occasional) and polyandry (rare) were also practiced. Divorce was uncommon but relatively simple to accomplish. Bride service, whereby the prospective groom lived with the prospective wife's family and contributed his labor and production to their household for a period of time, was the common practice. Perhaps for this reason, Russian observers believed that Koniag parents valued daughters as much, if not more, than sons.

Both fathers and mother's brothers (uncles) played important roles

Alutiiq Knowledge Specialists

Among the Alutiiq, "knowledge specialists" were present whose expertise covered different domains such as medicinal healing, divination, marshaling spiritual forces, and maintaining social order.

Apparently unique among Alaska Natives, Koniag Alutiiq communities had persons known as "wise men" (Koniag–*kas'at*), revered elders who were the ritual leaders of the winter masked ceremonials. Observers of these events noted that kas'at instructed the participants in practice prior to public performances, coordinated the activities of different dances, and essentially ran the entire performance. They were also poets and songwriters. As bearers of the cosmological truths, kas'at were capable of communicating with the most powerful spirits as well as with the spirits of the animals. They were also looked to for advice and arbitration of disagreements in daily life. For Koniag Alutiiq, kas'at influence and capabilities were viewed as separate from, superior to and more important than the shamans (Koniag–*kaliak*).

The shaman was an important figure here as in other parts of Alaska. Kalalik, both men and women, had spiritual assistants whose powers they called upon to predict the outcome of hunts, battles and travels, and to discern and endeavor to alter weather, prevent calamities, and heal certain kinds of sickness. Some sources suggest that certain shamans obtained powers from evil spirits and that "bad" shamans used their powers to bring harm to humans. Shamanic powers were activated spiritually through unusual clothing, facial painting, special objects, rattles, whistles, song, dance, gestures, and formulaic verbalizations. The Koniag whaler (Koniag–*arwarsulek*), discussed elsewhere in the text, was considered a type of shaman.

Shamans were highly competitive and sought to demonstrate the superiority of their powers over their rivals. In one famous encounter, an upstart shaman from the Alaska Peninsula undertook to test himself against the most renowned of Koniag shamans, Abshala. The challenger traveled to the spiritually-significant Augustine Island, an active volcano located in lower Cook Inlet, where he found Abshala. In a kazhim on the island, Abshala was ultimately victorious as his spectacular display of fiery rockets overwhelmed the rival, forcing him to admit defeat and depart.

Another category of "knowledge specialist" was the medicinal curer who utilized a diverse array of more physically-based techniques in their healing practices and passed their knowledge on to descendants. Included in the repertoires of these healers were herbs for beverages, foods and poultices, acupuncture, blood letting, surgical procedures and bone setting.

In Koniag oral traditions involving interactions between kas'aq and kaliak, the superiority of the kas'aq shines through, in part due to their consistent benevolence. Following the coming of the Russian Orthodox clergy to Kodiak, the term kas'aq was extended to them and the clerics gradually took over these functions in Koniag Alutiiq communities perhaps due as much to their advocacy for Alutiiq welfare as to their religious practice in the upbringing of their sons and nephews. Fathers sponsored their sons to be admitted into the collective of the adult males of the kazhim. Fathers, supported by their kinsmen, were responsible for hosting the feast and distributing food and gifts to guests who were invited to witness the ceremonial transformation of a young man after a successful sea lion or bear hunt.

Young women were trained at home by their mothers and her relatives. At her first menses, a young woman was secluded in a corner of the house or in a separate tent structure for a period of time. During the seclusion, she received focused training on her physical transformation, on the behavioral taboos and requirements during her menstrual period, on technical skills for processing skins and food, making clothing, and sewing the skins for the baidarkas and baidars. At the conclusion of her seclusion and training, a ceremonial recognition of her change of state was held in the kazhim usually incorporated into one of the fall ceremonial feasts.

Among the Alutiiq, gender roles for men as women and women as men were both recognized. A father was able to have a daughter raised as a man admitted to the men's house by distributing three times the normal quantity of goods on the occasion of being accepted into the kazhim.

Clear social strata are identifiable in both Koniag and Chugach society. The families who owned and headed the household made up a "noble" segment who organized production, oversaw distribution, acquired and distributed exotic goods through trade, and were major figures in the ceremonial activities of the community. The majority of the society, mostly younger or extended relatives, were commoners, the major workforce of the communities. The Koniag also held a substantial number of *kaiurs* (slaves), who consisted primarily of women and young people captured in raids or battles. These persons were responsible for the more onerous of the daily tasks such as acquiring wood and water, attending to the hearth, and answering to the needs of the nobles. They could be traded or killed by their owners.

Political Organization

Political practice in pre-contact Alutiiq society is another area where information is relatively limited and uncertain. Among the Koniag, the heads of households in a community comprised an informal executive council apparently headed by the most senior, experienced, or authoritative members. In addition, all adult males constituted a body that made decisions about relations with other Koniag groups. Finally, all adult males and females apparently comprised an assembly that met in the kazhim in the spring to discuss deployment to seasonal camps and production levels for the economic season with an eye toward possible

The Koniag used small carved wooden dolls for several purposes. These may have been used in ceremonial performances or attached to dance masks. (ALUTIIQ MUSEUM/ARTIFACTS OWNED BY KONIAG INC.)

upcoming ceremonies in the fall. After returning to the villages in the fall, a similar adult assembly would be held to inventory production, identify ceremonies, assume task responsibilities, and coordinate travel and visiting arrangements.

Trade and warfare

Trade was a significant aspect of Koniag and Chugach cultural practice. In the Koniag case this primarily involved traveling to the Alaska Peninsula or northeast to Prince William Sound. Caribou skins for high status male clothing and other furs were also obtained in exchange for whale products. Trade with the Chugach brought distant goods such as copper and dentalium to the Koniag. The Chugach traded with the Atna' for furs and copper, often using their Eyak neighbors as middlemen.

Warfare was a significant part of the cultural landscape among both the Koniag and Chugach. Among the Chugach, parties of men in baidarkas would travel to specific communities elsewhere in the sound to mete out damage. Koniag military apparatus included slat and hide armor, plank shields, and larger skin and wood protective frames. The Koniag were reported by Russian sources to have traditionally tortured some male captives prior to killing them.

Oral traditions from both groups testify to substantial conflicts internally among the sociopolitical groups that were motivated by a variety of insults or violations of agreements.

There are also oral traditions concerning conflict with non-Alutiiq neighbors as well. Koniag waged war with the Unangan with large baidarka flotillas from both groups periodically venturing into the territory of the other. The Koniag also raided Alaska Peninsula Alutiiq as well as Dena'ina villages on the west side of Cook Inlet. The Chugach battled with the Atna' and also with the Dena'ina. The most significant neighbor for the Chugach was the Eyak who occupied the coastal region to the east. While there was conflict between the two groups, the Eyak were both buffer between and trading intermediary for the Chugach with the Tlingit from southeast Alaska. Chugach and Koniag Alutiiq were on good terms and traveled back and forth between the two areas.

Despite the traditions of warfare, it was not a central focus of Alutiiq society. For example, no specialized warrior role or warfare leader is cited by either group and there are no accounts of efforts to capture territory or extinguish other social groups.

Beliefs

Koniag Alutiiq cosmology was elaborate consisting of origin accounts involving a primeval sun-man, accounts of spiritual forces, and numerous oral texts about how the universe functioned and how humans were supposed to behave. The purest of being, *llam sua*, lived in the sky. The concept of sua indicates the sensate, intelligent, volitional force of a form, its "person."   The universe was conceived to be hierarchically-organized planes of existence with five levels above the world and five levels below the world. Both good and evil spirits existed. A central premise of existence was that of spiritual recycling between planes and the management of the boundaries and pathways for appearance into this plane of existence.

Ceremonies

Central to the religious practices of the Alutiiq were the masked winter dances and ritual performances conducted in the kazhim. A primary focus of these activities was to thank and show respect to spirits controlling the availability and abundance of game. Some representations were of specific experiences of hunters. Among the Koniag and lower Kenai Peninsula Alutiiq, dances to mollify evil spirits were a part of the ceremonies.

Alutiiq masks were the presence and embodi-

Alutiiq masks were essential to the conduct of ritual dances and performances indicating the presence of powerful spiritual forces among the people. A wide variety of masks were used indicating the richness of the spiritual consciousness of the Alutiiq. (ALUTIIQ MUSEUM/ ARTIFACT OWNED BY KONIAG INC.)

ment of spiritual forces. They have a distinctive appearance with a long axis from top to bottom and a tripartite division into top, middle and bottom like a human face. Some masks are symmetrical in design while others have a bilateral asymmetry in terms of coloring or features representated (mouth, nose). A variety of types and sizes existed which could be worn on the head, held in the hand or mouth, or carried.

Accounts indicate that masked performances could go on for several days. Presentations included dramatic appearances and disappearances from the smokehole in the ceiling. There may have been a liturgical order to certain of the presentations referred to as the "six-day mystery" by one scholar.

Eyak

The Eyak, speakers of a language distantly related to the Athabaskan languages spoken in the interior, lived along the coast from Eyak Lake eastward to Icy Cape. During the historic period, they were primarily riverine people who had several villages in the Copper River delta among which they traveled in small dugout canoes. Squeezed between the expanding Tlingit to the east, the Chugach on the west and the Atna' to the north, the Eyak nevertheless retained an important position as middlemen and traders between these groups until the late 19th century. When the commercial salmon industry landed in the vicinity of their settlements in the 1890s, disease and exploitation soon devastated the remaining Eyak.

European Contact

European interaction with Alutiiq populations began in the middle of the 18th century when they became aware of the Russian presence and subjugation of the Unangan. The Russians endeavored to penetrate Koniag Alutiiq territory as early as 1763 but were effectively rebuffed for 20 years. In 1784from Vancouver Island, the Russian Shelekhov mounted a sizable force and occupied Three Saints Bay on the southwest corner of Kodiak Island. Following a devastating shelling of Refuge Rock where many Alutiiq had retreated, the Koniag were defeated and many hostages taken. In the aftermath, Russians began asserting total control over Koniag life, acquiring hostages and requiring males to hunt sea otter, often in distant waters. The Chugach Alutiiq, initially contacted by Captain Cook came under Russian subjugation led by Baranov in 1792. The vast majority of Chugach moved to Nuchek on Hinchinbrook Island where they remained until the transfer of Alaska from Russia to the United States in 1867. At that time, Chugach began to reoccupy many of their ancestral villages around Prince William Sound and the lower Kenai Peninsula.

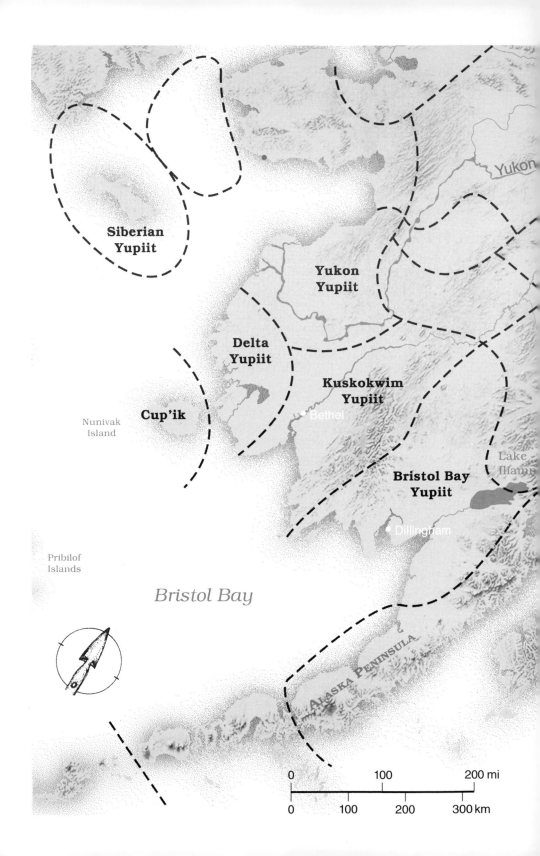

Among the Yupiit, young boys entered the men's house when they were about 10 years old. Here they learned the hunting and tool-making skills they would need as adults. Photo taken about 1905. (ANCHORAGE MUSEUM OF HISTORY AND ART)

Yupiit
Bering Sea Eskimos

CHAPTER 4

Yupiit

Bering Sea Eskimos

Kashim at St. Michael, about 1880

The term Yupiit refers to the speakers of languages in the Yup'ik group of the EskaAleut language family. Included in this group are the Siberian Yup'ik speakers of St. Lawrence Island (and several communities on the Chukchi Peninsula across the Bering Strait), the Central Yup'ik speakers of the Bering Sea coast from Norton Sound south to the Alaska Peninsula and up the Yukon (Kwikpak), Kuskokwim and Nushagak Rivers. There are four distinguishable dialects of Central Yup'ik; on Nunivak Island, local people refer to themselves as Cup'ik to highlight their cultural and linguistic distinctiveness. Alutiiq, the third Yup'ik language in Alaska, is spoken almost solely by people living on the Pacific Ocean (Gulf of Alaska) coast and are discussed in the previous chapter.

Taken together, the Yupiit are the most culturally-diverse group of Alaskan Natives based on the variety of distinct environments to which they have adapted. Siberian Yup'ik living in the middle of the Bering Sea developed cultural practices that were influenced both by their focus on large sea-mammal hunting for food and materials and by their interaction with the Asiatic reindeer-herding people known as the Chukchi.

Social units known as societies or nations among the Yupiit consist of a named group of closely related and intermarrying extended families comprising several communities with a common territory. This grouping was designated with the suffix *miut* attached to a stem indicating a location or distinctive cultural practice. For example, the Sivuqaqmiut are the Siberian Yup'ik residents of St. Lawrence Island while the Qaluyarmiut (people of the net) are the Central Yup'ik residents of Nelson Island whose expertise in making small nets to capture herring was well-known to surrounding societies. The suffix miut is flexible and can be applied to residents of a single village or a seasonal camp so its primary meaning, "residents of," can be used in a three-tier terminology from camp, to village, to regional group.

There were approximately 20 Central Yup'ik regional groups at the time of contact. Prior to depopulation in the mid-19th century, Central Yup'ik groups occupied the entire southern and eastern shores of Norton Sound southward to the vicinity of Naknek in Bristol Bay. The Siberian Yup'ik of St. Lawrence Island had approximately 15 winter villages organized into several local groups at the time of contact.

Archaeological evidence

The oldest sites in the region presently are found on the north side of the Alaska Peninsula along the Brooks and Naknek rivers dating back to approximately 9,000 ya (years ago). Arctic Small Tool Tradition materials including the oldest identifiable houses in the region date to 4,200 ya in Norton Sound but are puzzlingly absent to the south except on the northern Alaska Peninsula. Very few sites have been identified in the Yukon-Kuskokwim valleys or delta region until around 3,000-2,500 ya when Norton Tradition tools and artifacts, including pottery begin to appear in sheltered locations with abundant local resources. Gradually residents appeared to have developed expertise in the diverse array of resources necessary to survive in the wet tundra lowlands of the delta where archaeological evidence indicates occupation began only in the last 2,000 years.

The archaeological traditions on St. Lawrence Island are distinctive from those on the Alaska mainland. Early occupants apparently migrated to the island from Asia about 2,000 ya based on Old Bering Sea tradition artifacts found in both areas. These objects indicate a cultural pattern already heavily oriented toward sea mammals with wonderfully-incised art forms on a variety of ivory objects such as toggle harpoon heads, needles, needle cases, throwing board, weights, and small amulets of animals. The technologies and institutions needed to capture large sea-mammals appear to date from this time period.

Population distribution and settlement systems

Community size varied dramatically between Yupiit groups. Central Yup'ik communities located along the salmon-rich Yukon, Kuskokwim and Nushagak Rivers might consist of as many as 200-300 members. Central Yup'ik groups located in the Yukon-Kuskokwim delta region stretching between the two great rivers were generally smaller, reflecting the poorer resource base of the area, and rarely exceeded 100 residents. On St. Lawrence Island, the ancient village located at the northwestern corner of the island where access to whales, walrus and Asia were high, housed perhaps 500-600 residents while villages elsewhere on the island had considerably fewer residents.

Settlement systems varied according to the location of the group. In

---

Yupiit Groups and Estimated Population at Contact

St. Lawrence Island	1,500
Norton Sound	1,500
Nunivak Island	500
Yukon-Kuskokwim Rivers and Delta	13,000
Bristol Bay	3,000
Total	19,500

---

the Yukon-Kuskokwim Delta region, several moves during the course of the year to acquire smaller resources were required. Spring seal hunting at the edge of the shore-fast ice was followed by herring fishing in a number of coastal locations, followed by moves to salmon or whitefish areas, berry picking areas and ground squirrel trapping areas. In certain areas, caribou were nearby and could be hunted in the fall. St. Lawrence Island villages moved to the ice-edge in the spring to engage in ocean hunting of large sea-mammals first, and fish second. Perhaps only one seasonal movement was required of Central Yup'ik residing along the salmon-rich rivers; they could commute to their summer fish camps but went to muskrat hunting camps in the spring. Usually only males made the trip to hunt caribou in the foothills behind the villages in the fall.

Housing

The Yupiit constructed a variety of dwellings, some of which reflect their contact with neighboring groups. Among the Central Yup'ik, the common house design was a rectangular, partially dugout structure about 10 by 12 feet. Most had the "arctic entryway" tunnel which trapped the cold below the living surface in the house. Where wood was abundant, plank walls and floors were used in addition to the four house posts and beams. Lack of wood may have limited Central Yup'ik settlement in the reaches of delta away from the rivers and ocean. Woven grass and bark or sod was used to cover the exterior of the house. The inside had a small, open work and cooking area with a central hearth at one end and a raised sleeping platform either built of earth or blanks embedded in the earthen wall of the house. Oil lamps were used for heating and cooking where wood was scarce. Furs covered the walls and sleeping platform. Floors were generally of earth unless wood was available nearby.

These small structures were typically occupied by a woman, her young male children and her unmarried female children. Husbands, male relatives and older male children would visit their female relatives.

Platforms provided a place for storing food and supplies throughout the year. Note the two sleds and kayak frame. (Anchorage Museum of History and Art)

All Central Yup'ik communities had an additional larger structure, perhaps up to 30 by 30 feet, known as the *qasigih.* This structure has been variously labeled as the men's house, the community house or the ceremonial house. It was first and foremost the home of a related group of males who worked, slept, ate, socialized and trained their heirs together. A large open area with a planked floor served as the workshop and living area where food and water were taken. One or two levels of benches were attached to the side walls where the men and boys slept. Tools, equipment and ceremonial paraphernalia hung from the ceilings. The central hearth area was covered with planks when the structure was used for community ceremonies, the only time women were allowed into the qasigih. The structure was also used as a steambath for the adult men.

Summer fish camps along the major rivers had substantial wood and sod structures similar to those in the winter village. Less permanent structures such as tents were used for more short-term camp living.

Other structures were found around the outside of these dwellings including platform caches for storing food and equipment, racks for drying fish, storage pits, and frameworks for storing kayak and umiak frames.

Storyknife
(yaaruin)

Elsie was excited. In a little while she and her grandmother were going down to the river. Besides fetching water the trip to the river meant that grandmother would tell her a story accompanied by pictures which grandmother would draw in the mud bank.

This unique form of teaching culture to the young, called *storyknife*, was practiced by mainland Yupiit grandmothers with their granddaughters. A small (4 to 10 inch), scimitar-shaped dull knife was used to draw pictures on a muddy, flat surface such as the bank of a river. These illustrations accompanied stories through which the grandmother entertained and taught the child. The knives were usually carved by a young girl's father and given to the daughter at a community ceremony. Standardized symbols were developed in different villages to represent houses, adult males and females, infants, and activities such as walking, eating and sewing.

Elderly Yupiit women recount that the stories they were told in their youth had important information about domestic activities (sewing, cooking, weaving) and appropriate behaviors (respect for elders, quiet, avoidance of dangerous areas) and about what would happen if they engaged in inappropriate behavior. A common theme was the grandmother telling the young girl what not to do, the young girl doing it and then something dreadful (usually death) happening to the grandmother. This training emphasized obedience, the interdependence of people and the responsibility of a person for his actions.

As missionaries and schools in western Alaska assumed the role of educator, the activity shifted to creative storytelling between young girls rather than teaching from grandmother to granddaughter. Although some of the older stories and themes about behaviors and values continued, new stories of make-believe kind and scary stories concerning monsters entered the repertoires.

Storyknife continues down to the present day as a form of play and teaching values in some villages but the competition from television and school may ultimately result in the disappearance of this colorful and useful activity.

At the time of contact, Siberian Yup'ik housing differed from Central Yup'ik. A yurt-like reindeer skin structure with six or eight sides had replaced the partially subterranean houses previously used. These houses, termed *mangyteaq*, were home, work-place and ceremonial centers for a group of patrilineally related families. Men who worked together as a crew under the leadership of an angyaleq in the walrus, bowhead whale, and bearded seal hunts, their wives and children comprised the membership of Siberian Yup'ik houses. Again, the familiar platforms and racks for storing equipment were found around the dwellings.

Food and diet

Local resources dictated some significant differences in the diets of Bering Sea Yupiit. On St. Lawrence Island, the focus was on large sea-mammals with walrus being the primary source of food, skins and other materials. The Bering Sea herd with an upper estimated limit of 200,000 animals passed the island on the floes of the ice front in the spring and again in the fall. Bowhead whales preceded the walrus while bearded

The Yupiit enjoyed the bounty of some of the world's richest salmon fisheries. Large quantities of fish were harvested and processed through relentless hours of work in order to sustain families and their dogs throughout the long winters. (ANCHORAGE MUSEUM OF HISTORY AND ART)

Hunting at leads (openings between ice sheets) was crucial to survival. Patience, stamina, strength and skill were necessary for success. (LOMEN FAMILY COLLECTION, ARCHIVES ALASKA AND POLAR REGIONS DEPARTMENT, UNIVERSITY OF ALASKA-FAIRBANKS)

72-71-3541

seals and other seals were also harvested and fish such as tom cod contributed to the overall diet. The organization of large sea-mammal hunting, similar to that found among the northern coastal Inupiat discussed in the next chapter, included formal shares of walrus and whale sections to the harvesting group and further redistribution of those portions to kin and in ceremonial contexts.

Food and diet among the Central Yup'ik was obtained from a multitude of less-massive resources. The astonishing range of organisms used for food and materials used by groups in the Yukon-Kuskokwim delta is indeed impressive. Several different subsistence strategies are evident. In the lower reaches of the major salmon-producing rivers, intensive salmon fishing was dominant and was combined with seals, marine fishing, and where available, beluga whales. Up the rivers, among the more riverine-oriented groups, a development of the last thousand years or so, terrestrial hunting of caribou and moose and snaring of fur bearers (such as the important ground squirrel) supplanted most, but not all, of the coastal seal hunting activities. Only in Bristol Bay and on Nunivak Island where walrus were predictably available did Central Yup'ik pursue these large marine mammals.

On the outer coast of the Yukon-Kuskokwim delta, seal and beluga whale hunting were primary. Seals were generally hunted from kayaks in the spring and fall but they could also be caught in nets placed in the ice in the fall as well. The small sea mammals were combined with fishing for a variety of freshwater and saltwater species (herring, whitefish, blackfish, sheefish, burbot, pike, and needlefish) plus hunting and snaring small terrestrial mammals. An annual run of eels was eagerly awaited by riverine villagers as schools rapidly moved up the rivers to spawn. Migratory waterfowl and their eggs were a critical resource in the delta following their arrival in the spring when food resources were scarce. Throughout the Central Yup'ik area, a variety of green, roots, berries and "mouse food" were collected and stored for winter use.

Transportation

The Yupiit used several different methods of transportation because the severity of winter cold produced frozen lakes, rivers, nearshore oceanic areas and tundra for roughly half the year. During the unfrozen times of the year, the Siberian Yupiit used open skin boats (*angyeq*) up to 20 feet long for hunting large marine mammals, and up to 40 feet long for travel to trade, visit or go to war. Hughes (1984) suggests that the kayak was rare and perhaps absent among St. Lawrence Islanders.

Among the Central Yup'ik, by contrast, the kayak was the central vessel used in hunting activities and also for transport activities in open water conditions. Smaller umiaks of 15-20 feet long were also found among most groups with Nunivak Island Yupiit using them for hunting walrus and travel. Kayaks were used for sealing and beluga hunting but also for tending drift and set nets used for catching migrating salmon. The nets were made from caribou sinew or willows with the size of the mesh varying based on the species of fish sought.

During the frozen periods, Central Yup'ik used small toboggans to transport kayaks and other gear. Snowshoes, likely adopted from Athabaskan neighbors, were also made in areas where deep drifts were common. Dog sleds did not appear in Central Yup'ik communities until after contact but several dogs would be maintained for security and assistance in locating breathing holes of seals.

Clothing and adornment

Clothing varied depending on the environment. St. Lawrence Islanders wore distinctive dark, reindeer-skin, hooded parkas similar in style to coastal north Alaskan Inupiat. Waterproof, walrus-gut outer garments were used when in open water while sealskins provided materials for boots, soles and mittens. Central Yup'ik wore a wide variety of garments depending on available resources and weather conditions. Seal, bird, ground squirrel, beaver and caribou provided the materials for pants, pull-over kuspuks and boots. Salmon-skin soled boots were a Central Yup'ik type in certain areas. The overgarments were generally longer and looser fitting than Inupiat garments. The cut of male and female garments was also distinct.

Generally speaking, Yupiit exhibited less personal adornment than their northern and southern neighbors. St. Lawrence Island men wore tonsured hair styles in which the top portion of the head was shaved bald while the hair around the bottom of the head was retained. Women on St. Lawrence Island wore their hair long,

PCA 155-70

This waterproof jacket was made from walrus or sea lion intestines. The model is that of an open, skin boat. (HUNT COLLECTION, ALASKA STATE LIBRARY)

either braided or down. Three parallel straight tattoo lines down the lower lip were common among women. Central Yup'ik adornment was typically expressed through distinguishing objects or patterns woven onto clothing. Nunivak men wore ivory labrets through pierced holes below both ends of the lower lip. Distinctive hats were also worn by Nunivak men. Nunivak women would wear small labrets on ceremonial occasions when a septal pin and earrings might also appear. Some limited forms of linear tattoos are also found among the Central Yup'ik with the perpendicular lines from below the lip down the chin among the women being most common.

Social and political organization

The Yupiit organized their social and political relations in a variety of ways. On St. Lawrence Island, patrilineal descent groups, termed "clans" by Hughes (1984), were the central kinship institutions. Clan leaders organized subsistence, trading, warfare, and ceremonial activities. Patrilineally-related crews conducted rituals prior to whaling and walrus hunting and called on shamans for assistance. Their wives carefully split walrus skin hides and sewed them on to the wooden frames of the open boats. A man usually married a woman from another clan following a formal gift exchange and a period of brideservice during which the groom worked for his in-laws for a period of time. At the conclusion of the brideservice, the couple took up residence in the husband's house. Marriages were alliances among clan groups in addition to being personal relationships between an adult man and woman. Among more powerful clan leaders, polygyny might be found.

The situation was dramatically different among the mainland Central Yup'ik. While descent had a matrilineal tendency in terms of marital residence and groupings, relatives on either side were potentially significant. Flexible bilateral principles of identifying those with whom one worked best on a daily basis were central to the formation of groups among the Central Yup'ik. A pair of men often bonded as partners for life as work partners and their wives would stand in a similar relation. The Central Yup'ik used the concept of *elagyaq* to describe those who were "of the same stomach," both sharing food regularly and being biologically related.

While social status differences in wealth and authority were clearly evidence among St. Lawrence Islanders, such distinctions were played down on the mainland. Among the Central Yup'ik there existed a strong ethos of egalitarian, community-focused ideology in which elders as a collective were seen as a critical resource for the welfare of all. No slaves or social recognized wealthy, powerful persons were found in Central Yup'ik societies. While leaders coordinated the construction and use of the qasigih, accumulated and distributed wealth, those activities did not result in hereditary statuses.

Warfare was intense among St. Lawrence Islanders and between St. Lawrence Islanders and the Asiatic Chukchi. Special armor was developed to protect warriors during battle. Although not unknown, warfare among the Central Yup'ik appears to have been reduced prior to the coming of Europeans by the practice of ceremonial competition through dance, a central feature of the Messenger Feast (see below).

Beliefs

Maskoid representing
seal head with
rising air bubbles

Among the Central Yup'ik, *ellam yua* was a universal cosmic presence who coordinated existence and established a basic ordering framework. Two additional notions were key to Yupiit beliefs. The first of these is that all living beings have a *yua* or spiritual essence that is sentient and volitional and human beings must maintain respectful relations with the animal and organisms on which they depend. The second principle is that of reincarnation or "cosmological cycling" (Fienup-Riordan 1994) of the spiritual essence, the "person" of life. Human yua were recycled into life through birth and names expressed the spiritual essence of that rebirth. Powerful spiritual beings called *tunghit* controlled the recycling of different animal, fish and bird forms and determined where they would go to give themselves to worthy people.

Young people were taught to pay close attention to their thoughts, as the mind controlled behavior and could have deleterious affects for others. *Alerquetet* were taught to boys and girls as proscriptions for appropriate behavior while *inerquetet* were the prescriptions against inappropriate behavior. Central Yup'ik thought emphasized the communal interdependence of behavior by showing how inappropriate behaviors negatively impacted the entire group, and especially those who are loved the most.

Ceremonies

The ceremonial systems of the St. Lawrence Island and Central Yupiit were elaborated in substantially different ways. Both groups had various forms of social celebrations to highlight significant achievements or changes in social status. Spiritual or religious ceremonies, however, had different foci. Among the St. Lawrence Island groups, virtually all spiritual rituals were oriented to insuring that large sea mammals were properly and respectfully treated so they would return and give themselves to the people upon their renewal. At the conclusion

Weihland Collection 5863

The Yupiit cosmos was inhabited by many spirits including those of the deceased. Spirit poles were erected by graves to keep the spirits of the dead who wished to be reborn from disrupting the world of the living.
("Memorials to the Dead, Kuskokwim River," from the Weinland Collection, Henry E. Huntington Library)

of the whaling season, a large community-wide celebration was held involving distribution of portions to fellow villagers. This ceremony clearly demonstrates the themes of sharing and reciprocity evident in Alaska Native life.

Among the Central Yup'ik a wide variety of both social and spiritual ceremonies have been documented by Central Yup'ik scholars working with elders. The ceremonial season was named *cauyaq* after the circular drum made by stretching seal gut over a wooden frame. Through the drum, the heartbeat of ellam yua was felt and it joined the heartbeats of all participant in the ceremonies through song and dance. The rich ceremonial cycle that might consist of as many as eight separate events, was conducted from the late fall to early spring. One of the most important practices was the bringing out of elaborate masks that embodied the tunghit yua who were honored by such representation. The song and dance accompanying these mask performances have been termed *agayilurarput* ("our way of making prayer") to underscore their nature of supplication and honor (Meade 1996).

One major ceremony found virtually everywhere was the so-called *Kevgiq* (Messenger's Feast) in which two villages of closely-related people took turns in hosting a large celebration of feasting, dancing, and gift distribution. The name came from the practice of sending a formal messenger to a village to present the invitation and indicate what special products the invitees should bring. These events were conducted at the village level (as opposed to the *kargi* level as among the Inupiat) and with an aura of friendly competition.

Among certain groups, social control mechanisms were built into Messenger Feasts by collecting embarrassing instances of social transgressions by members of the invited village and poking fun at them through dances. This indicated to all present what the norms of the group were and the shame that could befall those who violated them.

Another important feast was the *Nakaciuq* (Bladder Feast) through which the mainland Central Yup'ik demonstrated their respect for the seal and sought to insure that seal populations would be abundant.

During the course of a year, bladders from all the seals taken were saved, dried out and hung up in the kashgee. In the winter, after new clothes and equipment for the coming season were manufactured, preparations were made for the five-day bladder festival. The seal bladders were taken down and inflated. Since it was believed that the seal spirits would return at that time to the vicinity of the qasigih to witness the ceremony, noise was kept at a minimum in order not to disturb the seal spirits.

The key element of the ritual was the belief that the seal spirit or life force was housed in the bladder. By killing the seal when it was awake,

B67.23.29

Masks representing animal and other spirits were an important part of religious ceremonies and dances amoung the Central Yup'ik. (ANCHORAGE MUSEUM OF HISTORY AND ART)

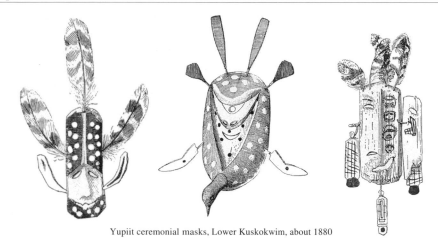

Yupiit ceremonial masks, Lower Kuskokwim, about 1880

the seal's spirit would be able to return in another body if the bladder was returned to the seal's home under the sea. After five days of dancing, the people took down the inflated bladders, marched to the nearby river, cut a hole through the ice and returned the bladders to the sea. The spirits of the seals could then return to their home underneath the sea and be reborn.

The *angulcaq* (shaman) had a special role for he was to leave the festival and travel to the home of the seals to see if they had been satisfied with the human efforts. After several days, the angulcaq returned with the good news. The seals were happy and would be returning in abundance. Through this ceremony the central Yup'ik demonstrated the mutual dependence of men upon seals and seals upon men for the recreation of life.

Contact with Europeans

For the Yupiit, contact with Europeans and Americans occurred at a much later time than for Alaska Natives living on the coast of the Gulf of Alaska. While more northerly penetration into Central Yup'ik territory by Russians did not occur until the 19th century, the lack of abundant developable resources such as gold, salmon, and minerals kept American presence to a minimum as well. The one area for which this is not true is Bristol Bay where the development of the sockeye salmon canning industry in the 1890s brought major social impacts and diseases. North of Bristol Bay, Central Yup'ik peoples have been able to maintain their culture, language and communities to a greater extent than other Alaskan Native groups. The isolation of St. Lawrence Island in the middle of the Bering Sea has also shielded Siberian Yupiit from major impacts of American cultural practices until the second half of the 20th century.

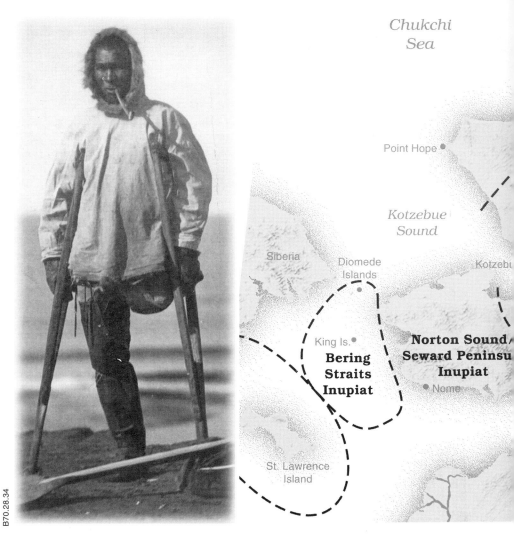

Chukchi
Sea

Point Hope

Kotzebue
Sound

Siberia

Diomede
Islands

Kotzebu

King Is.

**Bering
Straits
Inupiat**

**Norton Sound
Seward Peninsu
Inupiat**

Nome

St. Lawrence
Island

B70.28.34

(above) **Photographer Arthur Eide noted on his 1910 photo that this Eskimo living near Point Barrow "lost his leg in the ice, made his crutches and does as well as anyone." Inupiat elders who could no longer assist in producing necessities were known to commit suicide by leaving the group in times of stress so that others could survive.**
(ANCHORAGE MUSEUM OF HISTORY AND ART)

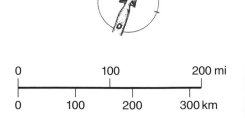

0		100		200 mi
0	100	200		300 km

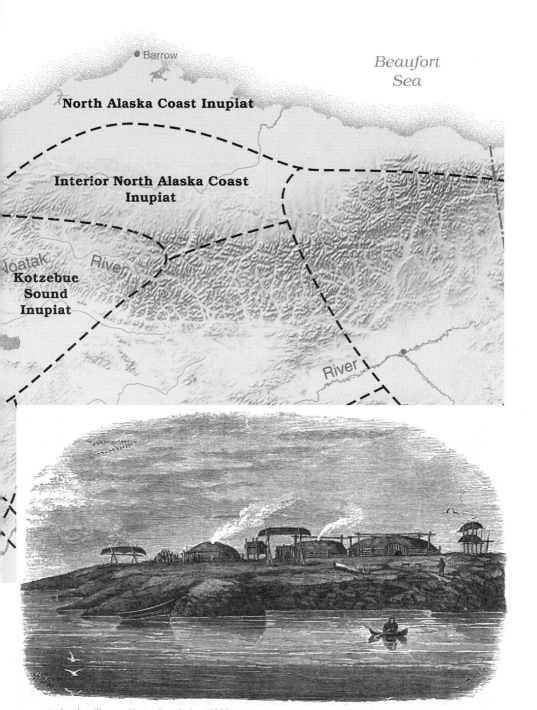

Barrow

Beaufort
Sea

North Alaska Coast Inupiat

**Interior North Alaska Coast
Inupiat**

Noatak River

**Kotzebue
Sound
Inupiat**

River

An Inupiat village on Norton Sound, about 1866.

Inupiat
Northern Eskimos

CHAPTER 5

Inupiat

Northern Eskimos

Walrus skin summer house on King Island, 1889

For most people, Alaska is the home of the Eskimo—hardy, ruddy-faced Natives who live in isolated igloos, wear warm fur clothing, use dogs and sleds to constantly travel in pursuit of polar bear while barely surviving on the edge of starvation.

As with any stereotype, there is a kernel of truth to this image but only a very small one. That kernel consists of hardy, fur clothes, dogs and sleds. After that, serious revisions are in order. For the north Alaskan Eskimos (Inupiat), there were no igloos (except in extreme emergencies); many lived nearly year round in some of the largest Alaskan Native communities at the time of contact; seal, bowhead whale, caribou and fish were their main foods, and starvation, although not unknown, was uncommon.

Alaskan Inupiat are part of a linguistic and ethnic population continuum that extends across the high Arctic from Alaska to Greenland whose success in colonizing this extreme environment has long captured outsiders' interest. The Inupiat, which means "the real people" in the Inupiaq language, can be divided into five main units: Norton Sound / Seward Peninsula people, Bering Straits people, Kotzebue Sound people, North Alaska Coast people and Interior North Alaska people. The latter two groups have sometimes been termed the *Tareumiut* (people of the sea) and *Nunamiut* (people of the land). These regional groupings are based on patterns of social interaction between groups that arose out of proximity, intermarriage and kinship.

The Inupiat recognized units that consisted of closely-related families of between 50 and 200 people who occupied and used a certain area. Each of these units had the suffix *miut* which means "people of." The larger coastal communities such as Wales, Pt. Hope and Barrow with 400-600 people actually consisted of a number of related or extended family units residing in close proximity to each other and in the vicinity of hot spots (locations where resources were concentrated).

Archaeology

The Inupiat region of Alaska is one of the most complex archeologically due to evidence of early occupation and the presence of several distinctive archeological traditions in the last 2,500 years. Onion Portage, located at a major caribou crossing on the Kobuk River, is a key site where stratified layers of artifacts demonstrate the occurrence of at least four different traditions at different times in the region beginning with Paleo-Arctic tradition artifacts around 10,000 ya (years ago). Occupation of interior north Alaska was spotty, sparse and intermittent up to about 700-1,000 ya when a more definitive Nunamiut presence is identifiable.

By contrast the sites along the coast are more recently occupied (since 3,500 ya), represent several traditions occurring at the same time, and, in more recent times, have larger sites with more people and more diverse artifacts. Between 2,500 ya and 1,000 ya, complex interactions among Asiatic, St. Lawrence Island, Bering Straits and North Alaska populations occurred as tools, artistic styles, and subsistence orientations emerged, were exchanged and refined. Among the most important developments was the appearance of a nozzle for inflating sea mammal bladders around 2,000 ya that increased success in large sea mammal hunting. The buoyancy from the air-filled bladders rapidly tires out sounding whales making their capture easier.

Evidence of significant contact between Asiatic populations and north Alaskan populations comes from the Ipiutak tradition, the largest site of which is found near the contemporary village of Point Hope. Distinctive burial masks made from assembled pieces of carved ivory, possibly the first large ceremonial houses, lack of whaling and iron set this tradition apart from those practiced by Ipiutak's neighbors to the north and south.

Around 1,000 ya, an amalgamation of tools, practices, and subsistence strategies based on the multiple traditions of the region was fused into a synthetic tradition called Thule. Both Inupiat and Yupiit groups north of the Alaska Peninsula were practicing a form of the Thule tradition at the time of European contact. Archaeological evidence from northern Canada and Greenland demonstrate that bearers of the Thule tradition expanded eastward from north Alaska and absorbed or displaced previous occupants of those territories, arriving in Greenland about 700 ya.

Population distribution

The population of the Inupiat is estimated to have been a around 10,000 people at the time of contact with Euroamericans in the 19th century.

B70.28.17

The Tareumiut, or "people of the sea," developed ingenious tools and methods for hunting seals, whales and other marine mammals. During the late 19th century, their resourcefulness and generosity saved many Yankee whalers whose vessels were trapped in the grip of the Arctic ice. (LOMEN FAMILY COLLECTION, ARCHIVES, ALASKA AND POLAR REGIONS DEPARTMENT, UNIVERSITY OF ALASKA, FAIRBANKS)

Inupiat Eskimo Groups and Estimated Population at Contact

Norton Sound/Seward Peninsula	1,500
Bering Straits	
(Diomede Islands, King Island, Sledge Island)	1,000
Kotzebue Sound	4,000
Interior North Alaska	1,500
Coastal North Alaska	2,000
Total	10,000

Settlement systems varied significantly among Inupiat groups. Residents of the large, well-positioned north coastal communities were able to reside in their villages for much of the year as major sea mammal resources were nearby, at least seasonally, and successful hunting allowed surpluses to be accumulated. Kotzebue Sound and Norton Sound groups lived in smaller winter villages, ranging in size from 50-100 people, and might move three or more times during the year to seasonal camps to acquire resources. The interior north Alaska people were among the most nomadic of Alaska Native peoples although some built more permanent structures at least at certain times in the past. At least some people from every group traveled for trading purposes during the course of the year.

Food and diet

Three major ways of surviving were pursued by the Inupiat at the time of contact indicating their ability to adjust to different circumstances. These were large marine mammal hunting, mixed hunting and fishing, and caribou hunting.

The north Alaska coastal Inupiat and the Bering Straits Inupiat of Wales, King Island, Sledge Island and the Diomede Islands depended heavily on large marine mammals such as bowhead whales, beluga whales, bearded seals and walrus. The Inupiat pursued bowhead whales and walrus when they migrated north in the late spring and summer following the retreating ice pack. If the hunt was successful, Inupiat men would not have to spend long hours on the winter ice, fishing or hunting seal.

Kotzebue and Norton Sound people and other Seward Peninsula people harvested small sea mammals, land mammals, fish and migratory waterfowl. Pink and chum salmon were available to many groups in Norton and Kotzebue sounds. Other fish such as inconnu and whitefish were also important to virtually all groups. Herring and crab were used by the people of Norton Sound. Seals were a critical resource to all coastal groups while groups in the river valleys used caribou. Caribou provided about 90 percent of the Nunamiut diet (Hall 1985). During the spring and fall migrations, caribou herds would mass together making it easier to kill large numbers. People took a variety of other foods including mountain sheep, whitefish, hares, moose, bear, ground squirrel and ptarmigan.

While technology and ecological knowledge were keys to Inupiat success, hunting bowhead whales and walrus required a sophisticated system of coordinated effort. Each of six-to eight man crews independently pursued whales and competed to be the first to strike one. A complex distributional formula awarded the first captain and crew a majority of the whale but the second through eighth crews who came to their assistance all received portions. The first captain and his wife then held a feast for the entire village. Thus competition, cooperation and sharing were elegantly united in joint communal activities that made possible sizable, sustainable Inupiat communities.

Tools and technology

Eskimos are rightfully regarded as ingenious technologists whose inventions made it possible to survive the harsh living conditions of the arctic. The Inupiat tool kit consisted of a variety of stone and ivory tools made for butchering, tanning, carving, drilling, inscribing, sharpening and flaking. One of the most important tools was the bow drill, used for starting fires and drilling holes in wood, bone, and ivory. With this relatively simple tool kit, the entire technological inventory could be made.

The most sophisticated technology was developed for the bowhead whale hunt and included toggle-headed harpoons, lances and lines. Floats made from seal bladders had special plugs for inflation. Other implements included scratching boards for attracting seals to breathing holes, bows, arrows, spears, spearthrowers, bolas for taking birds, and a variety of snares. Fishing gear included nets, traps made of branches and roots, spears and hooks. The Nunamiut constructed long funnel-

B72.97.1

Umiaks could be used for many purposes other than travel. This one is helping to dry laundry. When overturned, they could provide emergency shelter from storms which develop quickly in the Bering and Chukchi seas.
(ANCHORAGE MUSEUM OF HISTORY AND ART)

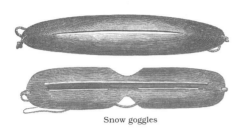

Snow goggles

shaped rock and wood fences to divert caribou into lakes or a corral where waiting hunters would kill them.

Another distinctive piece of equipment were goggles that protected the hunter's eyes from the powerful glare of the sun on snow or water.

Transportation

Another key item in the successful adaptation of the coastal peoples was the *umiak*, or large open skin boat. Most boats were 15-20 feet long, but Burch (1985) reports some nearly 50 feet long from the Kotzebue area. Six-to eight bearded seal skins were stitched together and carefully lashed to a wooden frame. Umiaks were used for hunting whale and walrus, and for travel and trading voyages. Large models could carry up to 15 people and a ton of cargo comfortably.

Better known is the *kayak*, or closed-skin boat, used typically by one man among Inupiat groups. These were constructed by carefully fitting stitched seal skins over wooden frames, leaving only a circular opening in the top for entry. Averaging 12 feet in length, Inupiat kayaks were shorter and stubbier than those used by the Unangan.

For travel on land, the basket sled was used for general transport and the flat sled for hauling the large skin boats across the ice to the sea. Dogs were not used with sleds until after 1500 A.D. Snowshoes were used in interior regions with deeper snow- fall such as the Kobuk River valley.

Clothing and decoration

Special clothing designs were developed to overcome the severe Arctic living conditions. Men's and women's clothing consisted of outer and inner pullover tops (the outer being called *parkas* or *kuspuks*), outer and inner pants, socks and boots. Tops and pants were made of caribou skin; the fur faced inward on the inner garments and outward on the outer garments. Hoods with drawstring were attached to the pullover tops which varied in length from mid-thigh to knee length. The woman's pullover had a larger hood for carrying small children. Pants, both inner and outer, went from the waist to the knee or ankle and were stuffed into boots which came up to just below the knee. Skin socks were worn and boots (*kamiks*) were constructed in a variety of fashions and materials in order to meet different weather conditions. Gloves were made from various skins with the fur turned inside; usually they were connected with a leather strip which ran around the neck for quick, sure retrieval if it was necessary to take them off. Sea-mammal intestines were sown together to create waterproof outer garments in the Norton Sound area for fishing and kayaking.

Eskimo clothing was eminently suited for cold weather. The bulky, layered garments provided for maximum insulation from the air trapped between them. The drawstrings allowed ventilation to prevent under garments from becoming damp from sweat.

House types

The design of Eskimo houses was also well-suited for the arctic. Although a variety of internal designs and materials were found in the Inupiat area, two key features were common. The first is the underground tunnel entrance which was constructed below the level of the living area so that one entered a house from below. This passage served as a cold trap insuring that cold air would not enter the living area. The second feature was that houses were semi-subterranean, capitalizing on

B75.134.1

Eskimo women and children, Teller, 1906.
(ANCHORAGE MUSEUM OF HISTORY AND ART.)

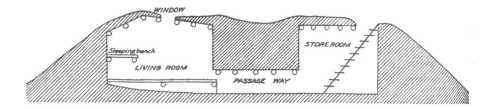

Cross-section of house, Cape Nome, about 1879

the ground as insulation against winter wind and cold. In most areas, the distinctive seal-oil lamp, made from soapstone or pottery, was used for light and warmth. This shallow dish-like object used a moss wick for burning seal oil.

Sod blocks, typically laid over driftwood or whalebone frames, were the basic materials for Inupiat house construction. Houses were generally dome-shaped. A gut-covered opening let in what little winter light was available and was uncovered for a smoke hole. The Inupiat house was rectangular, about 12-15 feet long and eight to ten feet wide and normally housed 8-12 people comfortably. The entry ways opened onto a general living area with floors made from driftwood planks or whale bone. People slept against the back wall on a raised wood platform covered with polar bear and caribou skins.

Equipment and food was stored either below the house in a food cellar or in compartments along the entry tunnel. Coastal Inupiat villagers laboriously chipped out ice cellars from the permafrost several feet below ground level where they stored surplus whale, walrus, seal and other foods. Racks and platforms for storing dried food and equipment were near the houses.

In summer, many of these houses became flooded when the ground thawed. This was not a great problem since most people left for the different seasonal camps to hunt and fish.

Inupiat communities also had *qargis* (or *kalgis*) which served as men's houses or community houses. They were constructed by an extended family under the leadership of an elder male. The qargi was used primarily as a work area to make tools and repair equipment but also were ceremonial centers for dancing and feasting in the winter.

Nunamiut Inupiat developed several house designs to accommodate frequent moves in different seasons. The primary winter structure was an eight-foot by 10-foot by four-foot caribou-skin covered dome whose frame consisted of an ingenious design of willow poles. In the summer, a triangular, tipi-like structure was standard housing.

The Frozen Family
of Utqiagvik

During the early morning hours of a winter night between 125 and 400 years ago, an *ivu*, a huge block of shorefast ice, toppled onto a house at Utqiagvik, near present-day Barrow. The sod-covered wooden frame collapsed and crushed to death five occupants of the house. There were four females aged 42, 24, 15 and 8 1/2 and one male aged 20 sleeping in the house at the time. Both of the older females had recently given birth and the 42-year old had been nursing at the time of her death. Neither infant nor husband, however, were found. We know that the roof collapsed in the early morning because the occupants had empty stomachs but full bladders.

The frozen family probably consisted of two related families. The 25-year-old woman is thought to have been the eldest daughter of the 42-year old. Analysis of the male tool kits in the house revealed two different sets of property marks used by men to distinguish their harpoon points. One set of marks is still used by Point Hope hunters today. The younger woman's husband likely was living with his wife's family after their marriage which Inupiat elders indicate would have been a standard cultural practice.

The autopsy of the two older women revealed interesting information about their health. Lines on leg bones indicate that periods of food shortage, probably in late winter, occurred every three to five years. The older women suffered from a heart infection, arteriosclerosis and experienced pneumonia. Many of her teeth were gone and those which remained showed heavy evidence of wear. Both women suffered from osteoporosis, softening of the bones, probably due to a lack of vitamin D in the diet. Both also suffered from severely blackened lungs due to the soot given off from the seal oil lamp. This was probably exacerbated by sleeping by the lamp and tending it through the night.

The Inupiat elders have returned the frozen family to their graves, but the misfortune of those ancients has resulted in fascinating scientific findings concerning life in the high arctic several centuries ago.

B65.18.573

Gambling was a favorite pastime of many Native men. These Inupiat men are gambling for walrus tusks in the shadow of an umiak.
(ANCHORAGE MUSEUM OF HISTORY AND ART)

Social organization

Kinship was the most important principle of Inupiat society. Among most groups, strangers were treated as dangerous enemies who could be killed unless they could establish some kinship relationship with a member of the group into whose territory they entered. As in modern American society, Inupiat reckoned kinsmen *bilaterally*, that is, relatives on both the mother's and father's sides were equally important. In fact anthropologists label a kinship system which uses the same terms for relatives on either side (i.e. uncle, aunt, grandmother, grandfather, cousin) an "Eskimo" kinship system. In such a system, each individual has a *kindred*, a group of related individuals drawn equally from parents, siblings and their offspring on both mother's and father's sides. These would be the people who would occupy a home or homes close together and with whom most activities would be conducted.

Given the danger of not being related, a variety of mechanisms were developed in Inupiat society for establishing quasi-kinship relationships. One of these was the trading partnership which was used to link together men from different groups who could then exchange goods. These long-standing relationships could include short-term exchanges of spouses as part of the generosity between the two families. Inupiat

Waterproof outerwear, probably made from walrus intestines and decorated with cormorant feathers.

(M. Z. VIROKOUROFF COLLECTION, ALASKA STATE LIBRARY)

who had the same name also recognized a relationship between each other. Finally, through adoption which was quite common, Inupiat children would be shared by parents with grandparents and childless relatives, thus extending the network of caring adults watching over the child.

Eskimo society has long been considered a model of egalitarianism in which all men were equal and judged solely by their achievements. Among the Inupiat, this stereotype must be seriously qualified. Although slavery and rigid classes did not exist, there was considerable property and wealth to be inherited in the form of boats and hunting equipment. The *umialik*, literally "captain of the umiak," was a substantial figure, responsible for many activities including the whale hunt, the qargi, ceremonies, festivals, religious rituals and trading expeditions. In Inupiat belief and practice, husband and wife both must carry out their spiritual and secular responsibilities so the umialik was worthy to receive a whale.

This unique and multifaceted role had both achieved and ascribed elements as powerful and successful whale hunters could attract a following from beyond their kinsmen. However, those who inherited whaling equipment and training had a head start in attaining umialik status.

Among Bering Straits Inupiat, a system called *ningiq* operated in the winter that required successful seal hunters to award a portion of their catch to any other man of the community, relative or not, should he request it while the hunter was transporting the catch back to the village. This system provided an acceptable form of communal insurance that did not compromise the autonomy of independent male hunters.

Male and female roles were complementary but strictly divided and hierarchical; males were dominant. Preferential female infanticide was practiced, but due to the many accidental deaths suffered by males, the number of adult men and women tended to be fairly balanced.

Women were trained in the skills of tanning, sewing and food preparation; wives observed many taboos and rituals to assist their husbands' hunting. These included a broad range of activities such as cutting skins at certain times, eating certain foods or looking in certain directions. It was thought that if those taboos were broken, then bad luck would befall the husband's hunting efforts.

Another stereotype about Eskimos is that they are cheerful, friendly and open. Burch (1998), however, suggests that there was a high degree of competitiveness evident in Inupiat society and that stress was placed on competence as well as being better than one's peers. Certainly one of the great pastimes of the Inupiat was engaging in a wide variety of competitive games which tested the strength, stamina and pain thresholds of the participants.

Within the local group, tensions between men could be controlled through the *song duel*. In this event, a man who felt wronged by another would challenge him to an exchange of belittling songs. The entire group would gather to witness the duel. The men would take turns singing songs which through wit and derision identified the wrongdoing or falsity of the other person. The group would respond with laughter to each song and the duel would continue until one man withdrew in shame. The matter was expected to be closed with the ending of the duel.

Trade

Trade was an important aspect of Inupiat life, particularly after establishment of Russian outposts in Siberia in the late 17th century made tobacco and other European goods available through exchange with the Chukchi. More traditional trade, such as that carried out in the trading partnerships, brought interior and coastal peoples together for the exchange of products. Seal oil and *muktuk* (whale skin with blubber) were prized by interior peoples who provided caribou and other fur skins in exchange for them. Trade fairs, attended by people from many areas, were conducted in mid-summer at several locations including Sisualik in Kotzebue Sound and Niklik at the mouth of the Colville River.

Warfare

Competitiveness among Inupiat groups is also evident in the frequency of intersocietal warfare. Pitched battles between groups with each side composed of a hundred or more warriors were not unknown. Particularly for Bering Strait and Kotzebue Sound people, territorial boundaries were well known and defended against interlopers. "Nations" from both regions engaged in serious conflict with Chukchi and Yupiit from Siberia in addition to battling among themselves.

Ceremonies

Several ceremonies were important to the Inupiat. Among all groups, the *Messenger Feast*, the practice of inviting a group from another area to one's home community, was common. The feast occurred in the fall or winter and was sponsored by an umialik who invited his partner from another group. The visitors were presented gifts when they arrived followed by several days of dances, feasts and games.

Several additional special ceremonies were conducted by the north Alaska coastal Inupiat to whom the bowhead whale hunt was critical. In the spring, a preparatory feast was held in which umialiks distributed all remaining whale meat from the previous year which had not yet been eaten. This was to meet the requirement that one should only take when one was in need and was a means of displaying the people's worthiness to the whale. New clothes and equipment were brought out because this was a festival of renewal, of insuring the continuation of life.

For the coastal Inupiat, the ceremonial known as *Nalukataq*, which concluded the summer whaling season in early June, was an enormous occasion. Umialiks and their crews arranged themselves around an open ground where portions from those who had successfully taken whales were distributed to others in attendance. Thanks were given by the umialiks both to the whales for giving themselves to the people and to the entire community for their efforts. The joyous exuberance of the blanket toss, after which this ceremonial occasion was named, is emblematic of the festive mood of the people following a successful whaling season.

Beliefs

The Inupiat belief system appears to have been based on the principle of reincarnation and the recycling of spirit forms from one life to the next. This was true of both the human and animal worlds. Names of those who had recently died would be given to newborn infants. Animal spirits were seen as critical for only if they were released could the animal be regenerated and return for future human harvest. Consequently a great number of special behaviors were accorded various animals including offering marine mammals a drink of freshwater, cutting the throats or skull to release the spirit, and taking care to make maximum use of the products. If the special behaviors were not faithfully carried out, the animals might not make themselves available again. Shamans had a special place in Inupiat society as curers and forecasters of weather and future events. Healers (usually women) expert in the medicinal uses of plants also helped maintain Inupiat health.

Contact with Europeans

The isolation of the Inupiat made them one of the last groups of Alaska Natives to encounter Europeans and Americans. Several voyages of exploration made incidental contact in the early 19th century. But it was not until the Yankee whalers followed the bowhead whale through the Bering Straits in the 1850s, that the era of sustained and substantial interaction with Euroamericans began for the Inupiat.

Several devastating epidemics swept through the coastal villages in the 1870s and 1880s. After the decline of the market for whale products in the 1890s, the remaining Inupiat were left virtually to themselves until the second half of the 20th century.

Athabaskans wore finely-tailored clothes made from caribou and moose hides. Dentalium shell necklaces, floral designs, beadwork, and ornate knife and rifle cases became important ceremonial garb after European contact.
(ANCHORAGE MUSEUM OF HISTORY AND ART)

Noata

Deghita

Athabaskan village on lower Yukon River, about 1870.

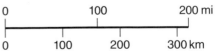

| 0 | | 100 | | 200 mi |
| 0 | 100 | 200 | 300 km |

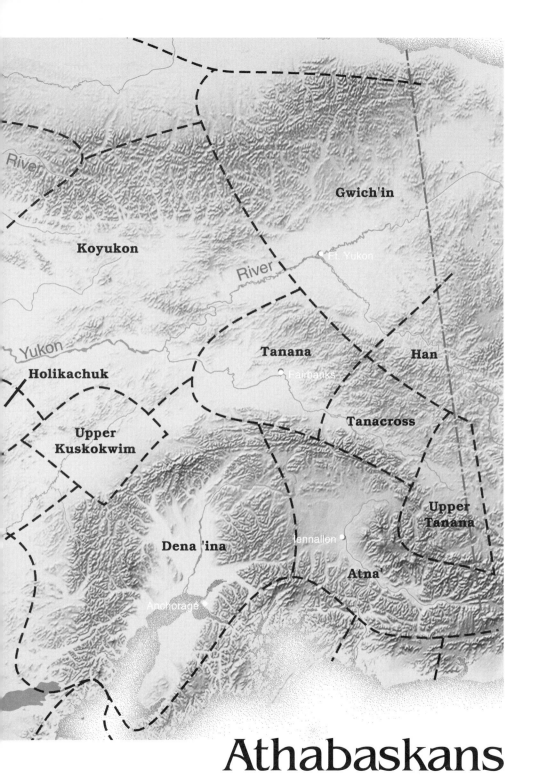

Gwich'in

Koyukon

Ft. Yukon

River

Yukon

Holikachuk

Tanana

Fairbanks

Han

Upper
Kuskokwim

Tanacross

Dena 'ina

Gennallen

Upper
Tanana

Atna'

Anchorage

Athabaskans

Interior Indians

CHAPTER 6

Athabaskans

Interior Indians

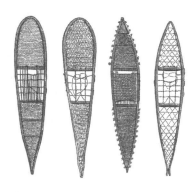

Athabaskan Indians occupy the broad interior of Alaska between the Brooks Range on the north and the Alaska Range on the south as well as the Copper and Susitna river valleys which drain southward from the Alaska Range. The only Athabaskan group to live by the ocean were the Dena 'ina who resided along the shores of Cook Inlet. Alaskan Athabaskan speakers are closely related to Athabaskan speakers of the Yukon Territory, Northwest Territories and British Columbia and also to the Navajo and Apache of the American southwest.

Interior Alaska, considered a portion of the subarctic environmental region, is bounded on the north by the Brooks Range and on the south by the nearly interlocking mountains of the Aleutian, Alaskan and Wrangell-St. Elias ranges. On the west, the transition from forest to tundra is the regional boundary while Alaska's two major rivers, the Yukon and Kuskokwim, cut through the region carrying abundant runs of salmon, with the Yukon continuing on into Canada. These rivers carry rich nutrient loads as well as substantial quantities of wood into the Bering Sea that contribute to the productivity of the marine ecosystem and the survival of coastal Eskimos. A mosaic of forested, rolling hills and wetlands predominate across the landscape referred to as the *boreal forest* that extends eastward into Canada. Soils in interior Alaska, having been spared glacial scraping from the last ice age, are generally more productive than in interior Canada where exposed patches of bedrock are common.

There are 11 Athabaskan ethnic-linguistic groupings in Alaska. Characteristics of these groups include similar language, *endogamy* (marriage within the group), clothing, ceremonies and beliefs. Each of the 11 ethnic groups are subdivided into units termed regional bands, and in most cases they are further subdivided into local bands consisting of between 15-75 people in several related families. Local bands were generally led by men who had demonstrated special competence in hunting, trading or organizing. Below the local band was the household level of organization which consisted of one-to three families sharing the same dwelling and basic daily activities. Among the more sedentary groups such as the Deghitan, Atna' and Dena'ina, the village was a recognized unit with a territory and a headman. Among Athabaskan groups terms of self-reference are identifiable by an ending such as *ena*, *ene*, or *ina* that means "people" accompanied by a modifier indicating their location.

Athabaskans are considered flexible and adaptive people who incorporate tools, social principles and ceremonial practices from their non-Athabaskan neighbors. Examples include the Dena 'ina use of the baidarka and kamleika adapted from their Koniag and Chugach neighbors for sea-mammal hunting, the Deghitan use of the qasigih adapted from their Yupiit neighbors, and the lower Atna' use of large plank dwellings and clan symbols probably adopted from their Tlingit neighbors.

Archaeological evidence

The Paleo-Arctic sites along the Tanana and Nenana rivers of interior Alaska are among Alaska's earliest evidence of human occupation at more than 11,500 ya (years ago). One of the interior's most interesting

B71.X.5.26

Athabaskans developed the cache to keep food and supplies safe from their dogs and wild animals. The cache is a distinctive Alaska symbol and is still in use today. Photo taken near Copper River, 1910. (Anchorage Museum of History and Art)

sites is Batza Tena, in the Koyukuk River valley, where for perhaps several thousand years, interior peoples mined obsidian, a volcanic glass important for its tremendously sharp but brittle cutting edge, and traded it widely.

The time period from 8,000 to 6,000 ya is considered a warmer, drier, windier period with lower productivity. Archaeological sites from this time are rare. Beginning around 6,000 ya, a new technology consisting of small, chipped stone arrowheads suitable for taking a wide variety of animals and birds appear and are referred to as the *Northern Archaic* tradition. While predominantly found in the interior of Alaska, Northern Archaic artifacts have been identified on the Bering Sea coast near Cape Newenham and on the Arctic Ocean coast near Prudhoe Bay.

Northern Archaic tradition sites have few artifacts and there is little evidence of wealth, ceremonial items or population concentrations, the lack of which are indications of a nomadic existence. Around 1,000 ya sites in Athabaskan occupied areas of the Yukon River in proximity to the Yupiit show influence of that contact in the form of ulus, pottery and ground slate tools. At approximately the same time on the Copper River, more permanent sites with house depressions and multiple storage pits make their appearance. It is also from this period that copper begins to appear in artifact collections used for arrowheads, cutting implements and adornments.

There are three views on Athabaskan origins. One view proposes they are related to the earliest Paleo-Arctic tradition bearers based on the similarity of technologies that change only minimally through time. A second view suggests that they were the bearers of the Northern Archaic tradition that moved northward into Alaska from central Canada. The third view suggests that the dispersion of Athabaskan peoples into Alaska and southward as far as Arizona is more recent and was linked to a gigantic volcanic eruption in southern Yukon Territory. A Gwich'in oral tradition states that the people moved away from a fiery mountain to their present territory indicating that some Athabaskan groups have retained a cultural memory supporting this latter view.

Population distribution and settlement system

The total population of Alaskan Athabaskans is estimated to have been about 11,000 people at the time of contact. They were relatively sparsely distributed and were most numerous in areas where abundant runs of salmon provided a relatively stable food supply. They can be divided into riverine, upland and Pacific subdivisions based on their location and their basic hunting, fishing and gathering methods. River-ine groups occupied areas with good salmon fishing, upland groups depended on caribou and Pacific groups took advantage of salmon and other coastal resources.

Athabaskan Groups and Estimated Population at Contact		
Group	Location	Population
Riverine		
Deghitan	Lower Yukon and Kuskokwim rivers	1,500
Holikachuk	Lower Middle Yukon and Innoko rivers	500
Koyukon	Middle Yukon and Koyukuk rivers	2,000
Tanana	Lower Tanana River	500
Tanacross	Middle Tanana River	300
Upland		
Gwich'in	Upper Yukon and Porcupine rivers	1,500
Han	Upper Yukon River	300
Upper Tanana	Upper Tanana River	200
Upper Kuskokwim	Upper Kuskokwim River	200
Pacific		
Atna'	Copper River	1,000
Dena 'ina	Cook Inlet, and Susitna and Upper Kuskokwim rivers	3,000
Total		11,000

Athabaskan patterns of settlement varied from sedentary to nomadic. Deghitan, Dena'ina and lower Atna' had winter villages with concentrated populations living in substantial dwellings from November to March. Their seasonal camps were often in close proximity to the winter villages, minimizing seasonal movements. Men could hunt in the fall on extended trips from the main village without requiring the entire community to relocate. A second strategy found among Koyukon, Tanana and upper Atna' involved smaller winter villages and three or more seasonal camps requiring entire families to move for extended periods. Finally, upland Athabaskans such as the Gwich'in and Upper Tanana lived in small, two or three family camps virtually year-round as they moved regularly to known resource sites or on hunting trips.

Food and diet

There are two basic emphases in Alaskan Athabaskan subsistence strategies. Among the riverine and Pacific groups, salmon fishing (including processing (drying) and storing fish for winter consumption) was supplemented by moose and caribou hunting in the fall and spring, and by snaring and trapping various furbearers. The upland groups who lacked access to salmon runs were more dependent on caribou which they hunted in composite bands coordinating efforts at key migration locations in the fall. Upland groups hunted moose through-out the winter and pursued a wide variety of smaller animals such as beaver, muskrat, hare, squirrel, and marmot; fished for whitefish, blackfish, pike, trout and other freshwater species; and snared or hunted birds such as grouse, ptarmigan and a variety of migratory waterfowl where and when available. Bear were occasionally hunted, sometimes for food, sometimes for protection and sometimes for the hunter to gain status. Members of all groups collected bark, berries, greens and roots during spring and late summer.

Notable variations on these basic patterns include the sea mammal hunting practices of the Cook Inlet Dena'ina, the sheep hunting prac-tices of the upper Atna' and the mountain goat hunting practices of the Dena'ina and lower Atna'.

Resources fluctuations are extreme in the interior of Alaska follow-ing cycles of predator and prey abundance or climatic swings. While a diet comprised of moose, caribou, and fish is excellent in supplying protein and nutrients, it is lacking in the high fat foods necessary to heat the body during the subarctic winter. A steady diet of hare or ptarmigan during the winter might lead to starvation if not supplemented by the beaver, prized for its high fat content.

House types

House types varied dramatically among Athabaskans.

The Deghitan, heavily influenced by their Yupiit neighbors, had semisubterranean log dwellings which had tunnel entry ways. Villages consisted of 10 to 12 of these dwellings, each of which housed two families, plus a larger kashim. The Deghitan settlements also had a larger community house, kashim or *qasigiq*.

The Koyukon and Tanana had semisubterranean log dwellings often built into the high banks of the Yukon and Tanana rivers.

The Dena 'ina constructed relatively semisubterranean dwellings with a tunnel entry. Inside there was a large central room with a hearth and several side rooms. The walls were made of logs and banked with earth.

Among the Atna', a variety of houses were used including large plank houses which could accommodate up to ten families. These dwellings had an excavated central pit area with a hearth. Raised platforms next to the walls were divided with bark or bearskins into separate cubicles for families. The Atna' also constructed a smaller house of bark laid over poles, similar to the dwelling constructed by their relatives in the Upper Tanana.

The Gwich'in used a portable, domeshaped, caribou or moose skin

Messer 14

Athabaskans lived in a variety of house styles. Homes could be dugouts, plank houses or dome-shaped caribou-skin tents. This photo shows an Atna bark house, about 1895. (ANCHORAGE MUSEUM OF HISTORY AND ART)

tent constructed by lashing curved poles together. The structure was about 14 feet in diameter and eight feet high. During the winter, it was heavily insulated with evergreen boughs and snow allowing the people relative comfort in some of the coldest temperatures on earth.

In the summer Athabaskans used a variety of temporary shelters including tents, lean-tos and smaller versions of the winter lodge.

Athabaskan groups used a structure known as the *cache*, a small, wooden house built on a raised platform, to store food and clothing and protect them from theft by birds and animals. Open raised platforms were also used to store materials and equipment. Another common storage technique was the use of bark and grass-lined cache pits placed around the exterior of the winter house. Dena'ina pits along the Kenai River used for salmon storage were over 10 feet long and five feet deep.

Tools and technologies

The Athabaskan tool kit consisted of a primary core of stone implements for cutting and processing wood, skins, and for making

Dog Mushing

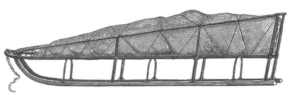

Deghitan sled

Dogs were domesticated in the New World about 10,000 years ago. Evidence has been found of their use in the arctic nearly 4,000 years ago. Dogs probably were first domesticated for warning and defense rather than for transportation or food. Archaeological evidence based on harnesses, sled design and whips indicates that dogs were not used for pulling sleds by Eskimos in Alaska until about 1500 A.D.

Interior Athabaskans placed 35-pound saddlebags on their dogs to transport their belongings. However, the Kutchin and other Athabaskans pulled their own sleds and toboggins.

In the post-contact period, several factors combined to rapidly spread the use of dogs pulling sleds. The most important was the establishment of trading posts (for the fur trade) and the introduction of the basket sled. By the late 19th century, dog teams transported supplies and equipment during the winter in most of northern, western and interior Alaska. This continued until the 1930s when airplanes began to displace dog teams.

The importance of dogs in the Athabaskan trapping way of life led to an emphasis on small dogs built for speed and stamina. These dogs have come to be called Alaskan Huskies. Soon races in the villages emerged as men competed against each other to see who had the fastest team.

Huslia, a small Koyukon Athabaskan village on the Koyukuk River, became the heart of dog racing in the 1940s, 1950s and 1960s. It produced a number of great mushers including Jimmy Huntington, Bobby Vent, and Cue Bifelt.

But its most famous racing musher is George Attla, nicknamed the "Huslia Hustler" whose life story is told in the movie *Spirit of the Wind.* Attla reached the pinnacle of his profession by overcoming a substantial leg injury. An uncompromising competitor, Attla also used modern methods of diet and selective breeding to maintain his team's position at the top of the sprint race profession in the 1980s.

As long as there are dogs and young men in the villages of rural Alaska, racing with the wind like George Attla will remain a part of their lives.

other tools out of bone and antler. All groups used chipped stone scrapers, knives, and whetstones. Adzes, wedges, and chisels were used in wood cutting. Projectile points of various sizes for use with bows and arrows show some variation; Atna' made some of these from copper. Especially well developed among upland groups was the three-to five-foot-long, sinew-backed bow which provided greater velocity and accuracy than the shorter bows required for use in watercraft.

Athabaskans are distinctive among Alaska Natives for their use of bark, particularly that of the birch tree, for a various uses such as vessels, bowls, receptacles and containers. They also used bark to line storage pits, to cover roofs, and to make canoes.

Athabaskans were masters in making and setting snares and dead-falls for capturing animals from birds to bears. Women were especially adept at snaring small animals and birds in the vicinity of camps. A variety of traps made from wood saplings or slats, stake weirs, spears, dipnets, gillnets, and hooks were used to capture salmon, whitefish and other freshwater species. At certain locations along the Copper River, platform structures were built out into the river from which to dipnet.

In areas where caribou were known to mass for annual migrations, Athabaskans combined into regional bands whose leaders coordinated large hunts in the fall. Converging fences, some miles in length, were used to funnel caribou into corrals where they were killed and divided.

Transportation

Riverine and upland groups traveled by birchbark canoes and mooseskin *coracles*, circular emergency vessels used for floating down rivers. Dena 'ina used kayaks or baidarkas.

Upland Athabaskans made exquisite snowshoes, varieties of which were designed for different snow conditions. Prior to contact, dogs were used essentially as pack animals. Tobaggan-like sleds were used to transport materials from camp to camp. Women assumed most of the burden of transporting goods from one place to another.

Clothing and decoration

Clothing was distinctive for its tailored, form-fitting, and finely-finished quality. Skins processed by skilled Athabaskan women were highly prized in trade by other Native people. Among upland and riverine groups, standard men's garments consisted of a finely-tanned white or light-colored caribou skin which came to mid-thigh; among the Gwich'in the garment dovetailed to a point in both front and back. Lower garments consisted of a single-piece legging combining pants and boots into a unified caribou skin garment. Women wore leggings and a pullover dress of tanned caribou skin which came to the knees. Winter garments

B82.51.12

Athabaskans generally lived in sparsely-distributed groups but in places where large salmon runs occurred such as the Copper River (shown here), large groups congregated. Dip nets are still used today. (ANCHORAGE MUSEUM OF HISTORY AND ART)

retained the fur which was worn next to the body while summer garments were hairless.

Both men's and women's outer garments were decorated with a variety of geometric patterns made from porcupine quills, dentalium shells, dried berries, and seeds. Fringes were also a characteristic feature around the bottom of the women's dresses and men's tunics as well on the shoulder in the back. In the winter hats and gloves made of beaver skin and fur were common. Infants were carried in a bark cradleboard.

Additional personal adornment was limited among Athabaskan groups. Dentalium shell necklaces, obtained through long-distance trade networks, were worn as symbols of wealth. Women might have three straight lines tattooed on their chins and men might have small linear tattoos on their arms symbolizing exploits in war. Nose pins were worn on festive occasions. Faces were painted, with red being the preferred color among riverine groups.

Both men and women wore their hair long. Men are often depicted with their hair down to mid-back with a neat pony-tail.

Social organization

Athabaskan social organization is a mixture of their own principles and practices adapted from neighboring groups. A fundamental Athabaskan trait bases kinship on matrilineal descent. With the exception of the Deghitan and one group of Koyukon, all Athabaskans

58-1026-2281

Birch bark canoes required skilled construction and were frequently repaired with patches and pitch. Smaller, easier to handle models were made for women. (Charles Bunnell Collection, Archives, Alaska and Polar Regions Department, University of Alaska-Fairbanks)

had clans, named descent groups into which a person was born based on the mother's membership. In the riverine and upland groups, there were three such groupings which were exogamous (requiring spouses to be obtained from another clan). The Atna' and Dena 'ina, who had 11- to 18 clans, also divided themselves into two matrilineal *moieties* (halves), known as Raven and Seagull. This is likely the result of contact with Tlingits who had similar principles of complex social organization.

Social stratification along wealth and class lines varied among Athabaskans. All groups recognized and valued the efforts of individuals to acquire wealth because it would be redistributed through the potlatch. The wealthiest groups appear to have been the Dena'ina, Atna' and Deghitan. The Dena'ina *qeshqa* ("wealthy man") and his wife were the leaders of matrilineal extended families consisting of several households in a village. Their status was achieved and depended on both organizational and management skills to acquire wealth through production and trade and open-handed generosity in distributing that wealth to their kinsmen. Among the Atna', a class of wealthy individuals might even be said to have existed. Slavery was practiced among a number of Athabaskan groups, but was almost incidental, typically consisting of women or children captured in raids from other groups.

Most marriages were monogamous with women marrying in their mid-teens and men somewhat later. Wealthier males occasionally had several wives and, among the Gwich'in, might use younger males to sire heirs by their younger wives. Among the Gwich'in, high-status women occasionally had *polyandrous* (woman married to several men) unions to brothers (Slobodin 1984).

Good hunters, traders and organizers achieved leadership and attracted followers, usually through kinship principles. They had little formal authority, leading mostly by example and persuasion. Nevertheless, there were some exceptionally powerful leaders whose influence arose from successful trading practices that generated wealth for their followers.

Warfare and Trade

The Koyukon, Gwich'in and Dena 'ina were noted for warfare. The Gwich'in fought steadily with the Koyukon and Inupiat while the Dena 'ina battled the Koniag, Chugach and occasionally the Deghitan. Dena 'ina villages were well hidden to protect them from attacks.

Trade was an important element in many Athabaskan societies. The copper controlled by the Atna' was highly valued by many groups. The Dena 'ina were noted traders between interior groups and the Koniag and Chugach. The Koyukon and Gwich'in traded with their Inupiat neighbors intensively after the 16th century.

Ceremonies

The major ceremonial event around which Athabaskan society revolved was the *potlatch*. The term applies to various formal occasions when one group hosts another,distributing gifts to the guests to mark important social events.

The most important potlatch was the *mortuary feast* given in honor of a deceased individual by his clan mates, usually a year or more after the death occurred. During the intervening period, close relatives manufactured and collected an abundance of blankets, other wealth items and food. At the appropriate time, an invitation was sent to other bands and clans to attend the potlatch. Upon arrival, the invitees received gifts in formal presentations followed by feasting and dancing. It was expected that the hosts later would be invited to a potlatch given by their guests. Gift giving was implicitly competitive with leaders vying to give more wealth and foods than their counterparts in other groups. The hosts were expected to give the very best and could be left nearly destitute after hosting a major potlatch.

A particularly distinctive event developed by the Koyukon was the *Stick Dance*, a marathon circle dance conducted around a pole erected either in the center of the village or attached to the center of a building. This was part of the two-day memorial celebration on behalf of a deceased individual but it also was a performance for all those who had died since the previous Stick Dance. Participants were exhilarated, exhausted and uplifted by the emotional outpouring that characterized the marathon dance. It continues to be held from time to time among the Koyukon today.

Smaller potlatches were also given to celebrate events such a birth, marriage, a boy's first successful hunt, and to rectify wrongs between groups such as accidents or insults.

A different but especially important event was the ritual associated with a young woman's first menstruation. A separate hut was erected where the young girl would be sequestered for periods up to a year. A number of taboos were imposed and she was expected to stay away from contact with men and their hunting gear for fear of polluting it. She was attended by a kinswoman past menopause who taught her the skills and practices necessary for the adult female role. A special feast hosted by her clan announced the completion of her ritual and her availability for marriage to members of other clans invited as guests to the ceremony.

Beliefs

Athabaskan beliefs about and relationships with the supernatural involved several important principles. A critical set of beliefs revolved around the similarities between men and animals in the distant past.

Both have spirits and in the past they communicated directly with each other. These ancient relationships had been transformed by the acts and antics of Raven, a culture hero and trickster who constantly disrupted the moral order by deception. The legend cycle, told in stories to Athabaskan children, is composed of tales concerning the activities of Raven, along with other mythical beings which exemplify concepts of right and wrong in Athabaskan culture.

Despite the transformations, important relationships between the spirits of men and animals continue. Especially important animals include the caribou, bear and wolf. Humans must remain respectful through ritual practices, such as sexual abstinence and taboos, in order to remain in the good graces of the animal spirits. Some individuals might obtain power through a special relationship with the spirit of an animal species.

Malevolent spirits must not be offended. One of them, termed the "woodsman" (or *nahani* among contemporary Koyukon), lurks in the forest to capture children and is believed to be what people who are lost in the forest become.

Among the Pacific Athabaskans, the *shaman* was an important intermediary with the spirits. Shamans acted as both magician and medical practitioner and could have either a good or bad reputation. Curing and predicting future events such as weather and hunting success were important activities of the shaman. Among the upland groups, shamans utilized *scapulimancy*, a method of divining the location of game when hunting success was limited. The shaman would place the scapula bone of a caribou in a fire and interpret the resulting cracks in the bone to indicate where the hunters should look for game.

Contact with Europeans

Direct contact with Russians, English, and Americans came rela-tively late to Athabaskan groups due to their interior locations.   In western Alaska, the effects of trade predated actual contact causing major shifts in village locations and the seasonal activities of the Deghitan and probably the Koyukon (Van Stone 1974). The Russian penetration of the Yukon and Kuskokwim river valleys in the 1840s set in motion major struggles over the control of trade which dramatically altered relationships among the Athabaskan peoples.

Introduced diseases such as smallpox, measles and flu differentially impacted Athabaskan groups. The Deghitan and Koyukon were espe-cially hit hard by the smallpox epidemic of 1834-38; some scholars believe this massive die-off led to the Stick Dance, a ceremony still practiced among the Koyukon today.

B75.134.10

"Horse Creek Mary" typifies the nomadic life of the Athabaskans. Women assumed most of the burden of transportating belongings. Many of the Athabaskan trading trails of southcentral Alaska became today's modern highways. (ANCHORAGE MUSEUM OF HISTORY AND ART)

Tlingit and Haidas began adapting white construction methods in the 1880s but the killer whale crest above the door indicates that this was a clan house rather than a private home.

(ANCHORAGE MUSEUM OF HISTORY AND ART)

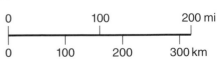

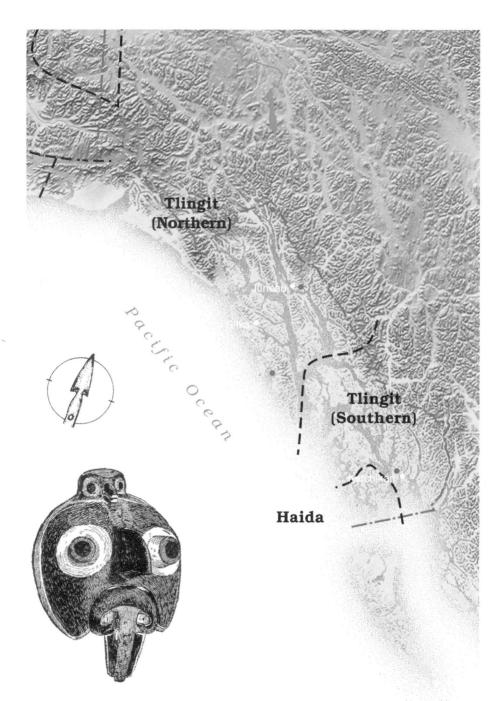

Tlingit
(Northern)

Juneau

Sitka

Pacific Ocean

Tlingit
(Southern)

Ketchikan

Haida

Tlingit and Haida

Southeast Coastal Indians

CHAPTER 7

Tlingit and Haida

Southeast Coastal Indians

TLINKIT CARVING REPRESENTING
BEAVER.

Occupying the islands and main-land of southeast Alaska are the north-ernmost groups of the Northwest Coast cultural region—the Tlingit and Haida Indians. They are well-known for their distinctive art represented in totem poles and other elegantly-carved objects.

The Tlingit and Haida are more simi-lar to Indians along the coast of present-day British Columbia than to other Alas-kan groups. The Tlingit occupied nearly all the islands of southeast Alaska and the mainland shore to the Coastal Moun-tains from Yakutat Bay to the Portland Canal. The Kaigani Haida, whose rela-tives occupy the Queen Charlotte Is-lands off the north coast of British Columbia, controlled the southern half of the Prince of Wales archipelago.

The two groups share many similar social and cultural patterns; however, their languages are unrelated and they have distinct ethnic identities.

Archaeology

While much of the broad interior of Alaska was ice-free 20,000 ya (years ago), the mainland and islands of southeast Alaska were covered with glaciers. Paleo-Arctic-bearing people migrated to the coast by 10,000ya. The oldest human remains in Alaska, dated to 9,300 ya, have been recovered from a cave site on northern Prince of Wales Island.

Archaeological evidence indicates that by 8,200ya, residents had developed a sophisticated maritime adaptation including the harvest of halibut, cod and sea mammals, and long distance trade of obsidian obtained from sources accessible only by boat.

Tlingit legends speak of migrations into the area from two directions. Some groups have legends of traveling down the Skeena River in north British Columbia and then migrating by boat northward into southeast Alaska. Other groups tell of travel over the coastal mountains or down the river valleys to the coast. The Kaigani Haida are much more recent immigrants to southeast Alaska having invaded the southern portion of the Prince of Wales archipelago probably less than 200 years before European contact.

It is likely that the distinctive elements of Northwest Coast culture— emphasis on woodworking, relatively permanent settlement, primary dependence on salmon, social stratification, wealth and art emerged between 2,000 to 4,000 ya in southeast Alaska.

Population and distribution

The Tlingit were divided into 13 units, sometimes erroneously labelled "tribes" (they were not tribes because there was no political unity at this level) to which the suffix *kwaan* was applied. This terminology defines a group of people who lived in a region, shared residence in several communities, intermarried, engaged in joint ceremonies and were at peace.

The total Tlingit population was about 15,000 at the time of contact. The most numerous groups were those living on the Stikine and Chilkat rivers. The Kaigani Haida population was about 1,800 people at the time of European contact.

The Tlingit and Haida had similar settlement patterns which included relatively permanent winter villages occupied from October or November to March. From these villages, groups traveled by canoe to separate seasonal camps where resources were harvested, processed and stored during the spring, summer and fall.

RBD 201-115

Cape Fox Village, 1899. (E. H. HARRIMAN COLLECTION, ARCHIVES, ALASKA AND POLAR REGIONS DEPARTMENT, UNIVERSITY OF ALASKA-FAIRBANKS.)

Food and diet

Seasonal food-gathering activities differed somewhat for groups who lived on the mainland from those who occupied the outer islands.

On the mainland, rivers with large runs of salmon allowed the people to remain in their villages longer. In the spring, eulachon were caught, rendered to an oil and then congealed into a grease which was a highly-desired condiment eaten with dried salmon or herring eggs. Moose and mountain goat were also available on the mainland and hunted in the fall.

On the islands, streams with smaller runs of salmon required greater dispersion of the population. Marine resources were more important. In the spring, people began by taking herring and bird eggs, followed by seaweed and then halibut. Seals were hunted at rookeries at various times. In the fall, deer were hunted on the islands.

An important backup food supply used in winter by almost all groups were intertidal resources such as clams, cockles and chitons. Whales and sea lions apparently were not hunted by either Tlingit or Haida prior to contact although both groups occasionally used beached specimens.

Food from plants were also an important part of the Tlingit and Haida diet. In the spring, early growth from a variety of beach greens was acquired and consumed fresh. Spring was also the time when women carefully pealed off cedar bark to make baskets, hats and dresses. They would also collect spruce roots for baskets and hats. In the late summer, abundant quantities of salmonberries, blueberries, cranberries, huckleberries and other delicacies were picked.

Many resources such as seal meat, deer meat, and berries were preserved in seal oil in bentwood boxes.

Tools

Major Tlingit and Haida woodworking tools included adzes, mauls and wedges. Carvers crafted sharp points and cutting edges from stone, bone and shell allowing them to skillfully fashion red cedar into everything from spoons to houses.

Hunting and fishing

Hunters used bows, arrows and spears for land animals and clubs for harbor seals (which were usually taken on land). On the outer islands, migrating king salmon feeding on herring were taken by trolling (a technique involving dragging a baited hook through the water to catch the fish).

Elaborate devices were constructed to harvest salmon. Semicircular intertidal stone traps were used to take advantage of tidal action; salmon would come in at high tide only to be caught behind the stone walls as the tide receded. A combination of ingenious wooden weirs and traps caught the salmon in the steams and rivers. Other techniques used to capture salmon included dip nets, spears and gaffhooks, the latter being preferred in the swift, turbid waters of mainland rivers. Men were responsible for catching and women and children for processing.

For ocean species such as halibut, cod and red snapper (a type of rockfish), the Tlingit and Haida used a composite hook consisting of two pieces of wood, yellow cedar and yew. They lashed a bone barb with cedar withes to the harder yew arm, then attached the hook to lines of processed kelp or spruce root and dropped it to the bottom of the ocean. A wooden or sealskin float bobbed at the surface when a fish bit the hook. Halibut hooks were carved with representations of powerful spirits

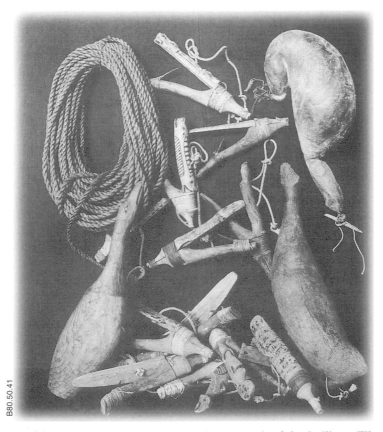

B80.50.41

A strong spirit was needed to overcome the strength of the halibut. Tlingit composite hooks were carved to attract power that would assist the fishermen. Lines were made of spruce root or kelp and floats were made from seal bladders or wood. (ANCHORAGE MUSEUM OF HISTORY AND ART)

called upon by the fishermen to assist their efforts. The hooks were designed to take medium-size fish, resulting in maintenance of the large fish for reproduction and avoiding capture of small, immature fish. Special clubs were made for dispatching the powerful halibut when brought to the surface where they were ceremoniously greeted and thanked.

Transportation

Yakutat sealing canoe

The Tlingit and Haida used two basic styles of dugout canoes for transportation. The Haida and southern Tlingit primarily utilized red cedar but in northern southeast Alaska, spruce or cottonwood was used as red cedar is not found in these areas. A small 10- to 16-foot model with a u-shaped bottom was designed for short, local trips and carried up to five people. Much larger canoes, ranging from 20-to 50 feet in length, were used for long-distance travel, transport, trade and warfare. These were deep draft, v-shaped vessels. Large separate prow and stern pieces were attached to the main body with cedar withes. The prow and occasionally the sides were carved and painted with the clan crests of the owner. Canoes were propelled through the water by diamond-shaped paddles which both men and women could wield superbly. Natives did not use sails prior to contact with Europeans. The Haida of the Queen Charlotte Islands were renowned as the best canoe makers on the coast because these islands had the largest red cedar stands.

Canoe construction was carried out by skilled craftsmen who identified trees with good grain, felled them and stripped the branches in the forest. Special thanks were given to the tree prior to felling and each morning the craftsman prayed that his efforts would be well received. The logs were moved by skids to a beach area where they were carefully hollowed out and kept damp to prevent cracking. The lines of the canoe were wrought by the fine eye of the carver. The final step involved placing water and hot rocks in the cavity and steaming the canoe into its final shape. The elegant lines were held by thwarts inserted at key positions. Canoes were oiled, moistened, and covered with cedar bark mats when brought ashore to preserve and extend their lives. Periodic replacement was necessary.

B80.50.25

Chief Sonihat of Kasaan presented this Haida war canoe to Gov. Brady and Alaska. It now rests on the green at Fort Chilkoot near Haines. Photo taken about 1904. (ANCHORAGE MUSEUM OF HISTORY AND ART)

House types

Tlingit and Haida winter dwellings were impressive structures. Their gabled, nearly square, cedar plank houses were as big as 40 feet by 60 feet, but the more standard size was 20 feet by 30 feet. Typical homes consisted of four large interior house posts, many of which were carved. Grooves on the top seated the massive beams which extended from front to back. Overlapping planks were placed on top of the rafters with a smokehole left in the center.

For most houses, the interior included a central, excavated, rectangular area for a large single hearth. At ground level around the outside of the interior, low-rising platforms served as living quarters. Bark mats provided screening for privacy.

The head of the house generally occupied the quarters along the back wall opposite the entrance. Twenty-to 30 people in four to six families typically occupied such houses and acted as an economic unit. The houses faced the ocean and were usually built in locations that were well protected from storms and had good beaches for landing and launching canoes.

Seasonal dwellings varied from simple lean-tos to small versions of winter homes. Among the Kaigani Haida, planks were transported from winter village dwellings to the important seasonal sites and used with house posts erected there.

Defensive sites, sometimes called forts, were common. These were typically located on steep promontories or islands where a group could

81.61.3

Tlingit houses were used for smoking and drying fish. The lip labret worn by the woman behind the fire was considered unattractive by European standards. (ANCHORAGE MUSEUM OF HISTORY AND ART)

go if they were under attack. *Palisades* (walls of logs) were sometimes erected around these sites to provide further protection. Smaller cedar or spruce houses provided shelter inside the forts. Clothing, tools and other goods were stored in bentwood boxes placed under the platforms and in the back of the house where the most cherished objects were kept by the head family.

Clothing and decoration

Everyday clothing was not particularly elaborate. In most seasons, men wore a deer or caribou skin loincloth. Women wove conical rain hats, often embellished with designs from split spruce roots. Women wore skirts woven from the inner bark of the cedar tree, a remarkably soft and pliant substance when worked by skilled persons. Cloaks made of sea otter fur or cedar bark served as outer garments for men and women, but neither normally wore foot gear of any kind.

Special clothing was worn for ceremony and warfare. A leader's ceremonial garb included a headdress with a frontpiece carved out of wood and decorated with abalone shell, sea lion whiskers and sometimes ermine skin pelts. White pelts flowing down the leader's back gave him an extremely impressive appearance. A small bowl full of white eagle

Totem Poles

TOTEM POLE, WRANGELL.

The totem pole has long been used as a striking and bold symbol of Alaska Natives even though they are only found among the Tlingit and Haida.   These exquisitely-carved sculptures in red cedar memorialized different events in the history of a person, drawing on the crests and images owned by his clan. They were not images of deities or icons of worship as a number of early missionaries mistakenly thought.

Precise and standard principles such as split representations of animals, form lines and ovoids created a unique art considered by the famous French anthropologist Claude Levi-Strauss to rival that of Greece and Egypt. The art form was also expressed in a variety of other objects such as masks, bowls, boxes, spoons and hats.

The earliest carved poles were probably *house posts* (the main interior supporting posts around which the wooden plank houses were built) or *mortuary posts* (erected in memory of a deceased clan head often having a niche carved in the back for placement of ashes of the deceased). These poles were usually simple, with only one or two images.

Metal tools and wealth obtained through trade with Europeans led to a proliferation of poles in the 19th century. *Free standing poles* and *portal poles* (forming the door to a house) with interlocking images and greater complexity soon became commonplace. New themes appeared too. Free-standing poles were erected to shame another person or group for actions like failure to pay debts. Even Europeans and Americans came to appear on some totem poles. For example, Chief Skowl, a Kaigani Haida, erected a pole with carved images of Russian Orthodox priests to memorialize his opposition to Christian beliefs.

The explosion of totem pole building ceased in the late a 19th century when the Tlingit and Haida came under the influence of missionaries. Many poles were destroyed or abandoned as groups left their old villages to consolidate in larger communities. In the 1930s a number of Tlingit, Haida and Tsimshian men were hired by the Civilian Conservation Corps to move and renovate some of the older poles. Totem parks were established at Saxman (outside Ketchikan), Klawock, Hydaburg and elsewhere. In the 1970s, the largest pole ever raised was erected in Kake symbolizing the resurgence of interest in traditional art by the Tlingit and Haida.

B80.50.28

Hats came in both everyday and ceremonial styles. The circles and ermine skin on top of the decorated hat indicate that it belonged to a chief who gave four potlaches in his life. (ANCHORAGE MUSEUM OF HISTORY AND ART)

down was seated in the top of the head gear. The feathers would fly up and drift down during quick dancing motions of the wearer and was considered a sign of welcome and peaceful intent.

One of the most distinctive items of Tlingit and Haida garb was the *Chilkat robe*. This was a garment woven by women based on a totemic design drawn by men. It was made from mountain goat wool and cedar bark strips. Fringed strands of wool dangled from the bottom of the blanket and dyes produced the standard yellow and black coloration. Robes were worn or displayed on ceremonial occasions and demonstrated the great wealth of the owner. Although originally developed by the Tsimshian, the Chilkat Tlingit paid for the right to weave the blankets and became specialists in their production. They were highly valued along the Northwest Coast and were a major trade item.

Special garments were used by both the Tlingit and Haida for warfare. Armor constructed of slat rods woven together or thick moose or elk hide were worn as chest protectors. Wooden helmets were also worn by the Tlingit. Principal weapons included thrusting spears, daggers, clubs, axes, and bows andarrows.

Personal adornment for both groups included facial painting for both men and women, and labrets and nose pins for women. Body tattooing was common among the Haida, especially for high status women.

Social organization

Social organization among the Tlingit and Haida was the most formal and structured of any Alaskan Native group. Matrilineal descent determined group membership, inheritance of leadership and wealth. Both societies were divided into two matrilineal moieties, Raven and Eagle or Wolf. An individual was a member of one or the other "side" and had to obtain a marriage partner from the opposite side; to marry or have sexual relations with a member of one's own moiety was considered incestuous.

Martrilineal *clans* were found in both groups; there were about 70-80 Tlingit clans and eight to ten Kaigani Haida clans at the time of contact. Individuals were born into these totemic corporate groups

B80.50.20

Tlingit and Haida artisans worked a variety of materials to craft a wide range of eleborate goods including baskets, bracelets, bowls, spoons, rattles, daggers, masks, paddles, hats, drums, dolls and Chilkat robes. The miniature canoes and totems were made for the tourist trade.
(Anchorage Museum of History and Art)

which traced their origins from mythical or legendary incidents.

The clans were typically named after an animal or mythical being. For example the Kiksadi, a important clan among the Sitka people, claimed the frog as its major symbol or crest. This symbol was used on clothing, blankets, poles, bowls, spoons and other property of members of the clan and was not to be used by people belonging to other clans. Appropriation of crests and symbols were considered thefts and could result in violence between groups.

Clans were the most crucial units in Tlingit and Haida society since they held ownership to property—houses, fishing grounds, canoes, crests, ceremonial garments, dances, songs and stories. Property concepts were highly developed and respected in both Tlingit and Haida society.

In some communities, clans grew so large that all their members could not live in a single dwelling; in such cases, multiple houses of a single clan came to exist. In these cases, each house was given a special

RBD 201-116

Prior to contact, Tlingit and Haida winter villages typically were composed of two to ten houses of the same clan fronting the ocean on sandy beaches protected from southeast and northwest winds.

Cape Fox Village, shown above in 1899, was an amalgamated village composed of houses from several clans. Changes seen from Euro-American influences include free-standing multi-figured poles, house-front totemic paintings, milled lumber and pillar-and-lintel doorways.

(E. H. HARRIMAN COLLECTION, ARCHIVES, ALASKA AND POLAR REGIONS DEPARTMENT, UNIVERSITY OF ALASKA-FAIRBANKS)

name, and the *house group* became the primary social unit in a person's life. The head of a Tlingit house was called the *hitsati* and was responsible for the well-being of all those living in the house.

Tlingit and Haida societies were stratified, meaning that there were clearly identifiable classes of people. Classes are usually divided into the nobles or aristocracy (*aanyadi* among the Tlingit), the commoners and the slaves.

Members of the aristocracy were the leaders of the clans and houses and acted as trustees over clan property for the other members. Young men and women of this class were taught special lore and behavior concerning ceremonial activities and their ancestral heritage. Typically long-standing relationships were established between two clans in opposite moieties who would intermarry over generations. This served to concentrate the wealth of both groups into a small group. For this reason, marriages, particularly among the nobles, were arranged by the mother and her brother for the woman's children.

One of the results of matrilineal descent combined with male leadership was the practice known as the *avunculate*. At marriage, a woman went to live in her husband's home. Her offspring, however, would move back to live with her brother in mid-childhood because the mother's brother (uncle) was primarily responsible for the upbringing of the children with the assistance of his mother. High status eldest nephews would likely inherit the position of their *hitsati* uncle unless they showed an inability to cope with the knowledge or organizational and leadership demands of the position during training. Eventually the younger brothers and sisters became the commoner class.

Slaves were fairly numerous and were important in both trade and providing labor. They drew water, hauled wood, repaired fish traps, caught and put up fish and otherwise carried out many of the drudgeries of daily life. They were also important at potlatches when they might be either killed or released.

Ceremonies

The major ceremonial institution among the Tlingit and Haida was the *potlatch*. This was staged with great pomp and ceremony, primarily to honor a deceased person but also to demonstrate the clan's status and the competence of the heir. Due to a combination of grieving and fear of the corpse, Tlingit clansmen did not handle arrangements for the interment of their dead. Rather the members of the opposite moiety, typically those of the clan with which the long-established ties existed, would take care of the body and details of the burial or cremation, depending on the status of the dead person's position. Most were cremated but shamans would be interred in coffins away from the community.

About a year later, the heirs of the deceased would invite those who carried out the burial work and other clan members from the opposite moiety to the potlatch. Goods, wealth and foods which had been accumulated during the intervening year were distributed in memory of the deceased individual and in thanks for the efforts of the other side. This event was usually staged by the heir and symbolized his assumption of the position of the deceased. Clan crests, dances, ceremonial bowls and spoons, and garments (such as Chilkat robes) would be demonstrated showing the group's properties and rights. Perhaps the most important wealth items were *coppers*, pieces of copper pounded flat and engraved with totemic symbols. It is not clear if such objects existed in the pre-contact era, but with the introduction of sheet copper from Europeans, they began to proliferate. Usually a *mortuary pole* was commissioned and raised during the potlatch.

Potlatches expressed strong reciprocal and competitive elements. Those who gave the most attained high status through the lore which recognized their generosity. This was symbolized in special potlatch hats with rings indicating the number of potlatches an individual had sponsored. Those who were invited guests at one potlatch would be hosts later to the same people due to the division of labor between the moieties and the obligations which linked the clans together.

Potlatches were held on other occasions such as naming ceremonies, weddings, house-raising ceremonies (especially among the Haida), raising special totem poles and eradicating shameful or embarrassing incidents.

Tlingit ready for battle, from
Harper's Weekly, 1869
courtesy Anchorage Museum of
History and Art, map 4/4

War and peace

Warfare was a common practice among both Tlingit and Haida. Motivations included obtaining wealth (including slaves) and righting perceived wrongs. Feuding, the perpetuation of multi-generation hostilities between two clan groups, was also well known. Most hostilities took the form of raids and ambushes. The Haida were considered the fiercest raiders of the coast, ranging as far south as Puget Sound in pursuit of slaves and booty, possibly due to population pressures on resources in the Queen Charlotte Islands.

Tlingit warfare was part of a system of justice that sought balance in the costs that conflict inflicted on the parties. A major mechanism used to restore balance was the *Goacan* (Deer) ceremony. This was a sacred ritual involving among several elements the exchange of high ranking persons from the two clans; their role was to demonstrate the dampening of anger and rise of peaceful feelings. The Goacan was conducted at the conclusion of a negotiated agreement in which lives or goods would be provided by one side to the other to establish equilibrium.

Trade

Trade was highly developed among both groups and was enhanced by the ease of long-distance travel over the relatively well-protected waterways of the coast. The Tlingit obtained caribou skins, clothing and copper from interior Athabaskan groups in exchange for eulachon grease, dried halibut, Chilkat robes and carved cedar objects. Haidas traded their famous canoes as well as slaves and dried halibut. A major event for both groups was the trade fair which occurred each spring at the mouth of the Nass River. Groups from all parts of the Northwest Coast traveled here to trade, put up eulachon grease, gamble and seek marriage partners. June was the time for specialized trading trips either into the interior along the "grease" trails or to other villages where specific desired or requested goods could be obtained.

Beliefs

The belief system of both the Tlingit and Haida were linked to the Raven, a supernatural trickster through whose activities most of the universe's features came to be. Other animals were also important as actors in Tlingit and Haida myths and legends; particularly important were bears, the Thunderbird and a variety of other mythical beings and spirits whose acts influenced human affairs. A distant powerful force of the universe was also recognized and individual Tlingits undertook purification and cleansing by immersion in freshwater to acquire personal guardian spirits to assist them in daily life.

Both cultures had a strong belief in reincarnation which was identified by dreams and physical or behavioral similarities of new born children to some recently deceased person.

The shaman (Tlingit—*ixt*) was a powerful ritualist in both societies who acquired spiritual forces (Tlingit—*yeik*) through fasting, abstinence and retreat to nature to assist in curing, foretelling future events, and of major importance, identifying witches who were damaging other persons.

Shamans were thought to travel great distances to see events in other communities and do battle with other shamans. They were well-paid specialists who had apprentices to assist them. Shamans, unlike other Tlingits who were cremated following death, were buried in boxes and accompanied by their spiritual materials, taken to uninhabited forest areas at a distance from villages and camps. Their remains were never bothered out of respect and fear.

Contact with Europeans

The strong organization and military experience of the Tlingit enabled them to retain their independence in the face of the Russian invasion of their territory around 1800. The Russians were able to establish a permanent foothold at Sitka in 1805 after having initially been driven from the area by the Tlingit under the leadership of Katlian in 1802. However, they exercised little military control over the Tlingit in Sitka and none over any other Tlingit or Haida group. An important element in the retention of Tlingit independence was their ability to obtain arms and ammunition from British and American traders who wished to see the Russians driven completely from the area.

B72.67.12

The Tlingit and Haida Indians were accomplished traders even before the arrival of the whites. The women adapted their basketmaking and trading skills to cater to the early tourist traffic which began in the 1880s in southeast Alaska. (ANCHORAGE MUSEUM OF HISTORY AND ART)

CHAPTER 8

Historic Change

Biship Veniaminov

Alaskan Native cultures changed slowly through the centuries in response to population increases, technical and social innovations, migration, war and trade. However, contact with Europeans brought dramatic and more far-reaching changes than anything that had ever happened previously. The Russians were the first to come, pursuing sea otters and the profits that could be obtained from trading the pelt of this beautiful and charming animal. The Unangan were violently subjugated and decimated by disease; survivors of the onslaught synthesized a new identity called "Aleut" by combining Russian and Unangan components.

After depleting sea otters in the Aleutian Islands, the Russians moved eastward to the Kodiak Archipelago. In 1784 they shelled the Koniag Alutiiq into submission and began colonizing the islanders. In 1794, a group of Russian Orthodox priests arrived in St. Paul (Kodiak) to minister to the residents. They quickly became critics of the brutal Russian American Company practices towards indigenous people and argued for more humane policies. A number of Russian Orthodox priests married Alaska Native women and descendants of these marriages are found in many parts of Alaska.

While the Russians were establishing themselves along the western and central Gulf of Alaska coast, a different pattern of development took place in southeast Alaska. In 1778 James Cook sailed as far north as Cook Inlet and his reports of the rich trade in sea otter pelts set off a mad scramble. English and American entrepreneurs sailed for the fabled Northwest Coast in pursuit of fortune. American traders armed the Tlingit and Haida, giving them the wherewithal to withstand Russian attempts to dominate the area. Although the Russians were able to establish a foothold at Sitka in 1805 after having been driven out by the Tlingit in 1802, they were never able to exercise control over the other Tlingit and Haida villages.

Sea otters slaughter ends but other trade continues

The maritime sea otter trade declined about 1815 with the extirpation of the animals virtually throughout their entire range on the west coast of North America. This resulted in a shift to trade based on terrestrial fur bearers such as beaver, mink, marten and fox. Between 1820 and 1840, the Russians gradually expanded up the coast of western Alaska establishing posts among the Bering Sea mainland Yupiit in Bristol Bay, at the mouth of the Yukon River and on the Kuskokwim River. Russian methods had changed by this time with severe terms of trade and missionaries replacing outright subjugation. But in the Norton Sound area, the Russians encountered an already-flourishing trading system centered at Unalakleet consisting of coastal Inupiat middlemen funneling furs from interior Athabaskan groups of the middle Yukon River to the Siberian Chukchi.

In addition, English overland traders expanded westward out of Canada and established a trading post at Fort Yukon in 1847. These competitors severely constricted Russian expansion and with the decline in the profitability of trade in the coastal region, the entire American venture became a financial burden on the Russian treasury.

The legacy of the Russian period included smallpox and venereal disease that wreaked great havoc throughout the southern coastal

81.61.1

New Archaengel (Sitka) about 1840. Litho by Fredrich Heinrich von Kittlitz.
(ANCHORAGE MUSEUM OF HISTORY AND ART)

regions. The Unangan and Koniag populations were reduced to approximately 20 percent of the pre-contact level while the Chugach, Tlingit, Haida and Dena'ina may were reduced by 50 percent. This caused a consolidation of the population. Intermarriage resulted in many Alaska Natives with Russian names. Literacy in their own language was created among the Unangan, Koniag and a few Tlingit through the efforts of Russian Orthodox missionaries such as Bishop Veniaminov to translate the Bible.

Russia sells Alaska to U.S. but little changes

Russian imperial disenchantment with the American colony resulted in the sale of Alaska to the United States in 1867 for $7.2 million dollars. The Tongass Tlingit group objected strenuously to the sale, rightly noting that the Russians could not sell what they did not own. But these protestations had no effect on a government and people bent on a mission of manifest destiny and the civilization of the American Indian.

From 1867 to 1884 Alaska had no civil government, first coming under the military jurisdiction of the Army and then the Navy. The outposts were manned by an extremely uncouth and rugged breed of soldier who apparently contributed substantially to the difficulties of the Native groups. One of the results of the military presence was teaching the Tlingit how to make homebrew or "hootchinoo." But more importantly at Kake and Angoon, Tlingits seeking to rectify injustices were given a lesson in the military might and will of the U.S. government. These villages were shelled with houses, canoes and other facilities destroyed. The independent Tlingit and Haida, brought up short by this devastation, realized that their days of independence were numbered and some form of accommodation was going to be necessary to survive.

A few whites from the United States began filtering into Alaska after the purchase, some as prospectors, some as whalers, some as store keepers, and some as fish processors salting salmon for sale on the west coast. These adventurers and entrepreneurs established new avenues of accommodation—trade and labor. Unfortunately, less savory traders broght liquor to Native villages, causing major problems.

In the far north, the Inupiat were exposed to Yankee whalers from the 1850s through the 1880s. This contact brought new material goods, opportunities for trade and labor, and diseases which decimated the north coast in the 1880s. The destruction of the bowhead whale and walrus by Yankee whalers combined with bad weather led to the starvation of 1,500 St. Lawrence Island Eskimos in the winter of 1878-79, reducing the population by 75 percent.

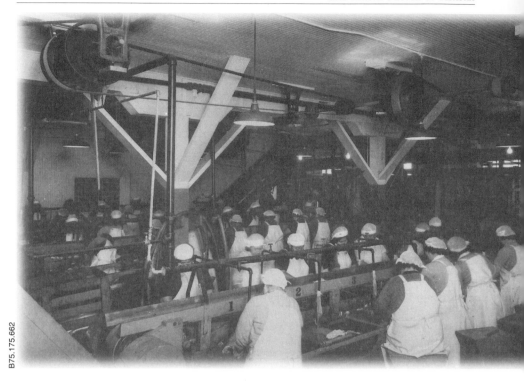

B75.175.662

Throughout southern Alaska, Native women provided labor on the gurry lines of many salmon canneries which operated during the latter part of the 19th century. Their husbands ran the fishing boats which caught the fish the women canned. (ANCHORAGE MUSEUM OF HISTORY AND ART)

Salmon canneries prove to be a mixed blessing

In 1878, the new technique of canning salmon came to Alaska and within ten years canneries were built on many of the Natives' most important fishing grounds. In some places the canneries brought opportunities for men to work as fishermen and women to work in the processing. But in other places, notably Bristol Bay, Natives were excluded from the labor force since imported Chinese were regarded as more tractable and reliable. Unfortunately, the cannery owners gave little consideration to the needs of the Natives and many salmon runs were devastated by the turn of the century despite Native complaints to U.S. fisheries agents. Although laws were passed to protect the fish, those same laws outlawed traditional Native fishing practices and subjected them to arrest by federal agents. Despite these problems, commercial fishing as a way of obtaining cash became deeply embedded in Tlingit and Haida villages by 1900, Alutiiq villages by the 1920s and Bristol Bay Yupiit communities by the 1940s.

*Missionaries arrive; English replaces Russian
language in schools*

Another avenue of accommodation was provided by the missionary educators. Sheldon Jackson was a Presbyterian missionary who visited Alaska in 1877 and returned to the United States with a vision of establishing missionary-educators in villages to carry out the Christianization and education of the Natives. In 1882, Jackson convened a meeting of Christian missionaries from various sects interested in proselytizing in Alaska and through mutual agreement, different sects were assigned to different areas of Alaska.

In 1887, Tsimshians from British Columbia, seeking a more congenial social and religious environment, migrated to Alaska and founded, with federal permission, a new community on Annette Island. Led by lay missionary William Duncan, the Tsimshians modeled a dramatically-different strategy for Native "modernization." Universal schooling in their own language was accompanied by collective ownership of transport vessels, a cannery and a sawmill at the village of New Metlakatla.

In contrast to Duncan and the Russian Orthodox approach to cultural change, one of the key elements in the American missionary plan was the eradication of Native languages and their replacement by English. Students were prohibited from speaking their Native tongues in school and were often harshly punished if the rule was broken. After the turn of the century, Jackson was removed as Special Agent for Education due to growing disapproval of the use of federal funds to promote religious schools and organizations. Nevertheless, his ideas and efforts established a powerful template in the minds of non-Natives and many Natives for how cultural change and development should proceed for Alaska Natives.

Natives begin quest to secure their rights

The gold rush to the Klondike, Nome and other Alaskan locales brought a huge influx of whites to the territory. The *Organic Act of 1884* recognized Natives rights to their homes and camps and stipulated that they were not to be disturbed in their use of those sites.

However, in 1894 Congress allowed whites to begin applying for title to business sites and many Native properties were taken as a result, particularly by canneries. Natives were not citizens and therefore had no recourse to obtain title to lands. The influx of whites and the inability of Natives to stake claims to mines further clarified their vulnerable, second-class status under U.S. laws. This led to a strong desire to obtain citizenship so that property rights could be obtained and protected.

In 1912 a group of missionary-educated young Tlingit men founded the Alaska Native Brotherhood (ANB) as a vehicle for achieving citizenship for Natives; the organization sought to eliminate cultural and linguistic practices viewed as uncivilized by whites. In the 1920s, under the leadership of William Paul, the ANB took a different tack, and began using legal and political action to advance Native concerns and interests.

The struggle for land claims was born out of the southeast Alaska experience. President Theodore Roosevelt had placed the vast majority of the timbered lands of southeast and southcentral Alaska into the Tongass and Chugach national forests. White settlers had established canneries and communities on Native lands.   This injustice led to resentment and conviction to regain what was lost among many Natives. Congressional legislation was passed in 1935 authorizing the Tlingit and Haida to pursue land claims.

Similar concerns were also voiced by the interior Athabaskan people in 1915 where they met with Alaskan Congressional delegate James Wickersham at the first Tanana Chiefs Conference. The chiefs complained about their hunting lands and fishing stations being disrupted by white prospectors. Other whites were trapping on customary Indian trap lines causing further economic hardship. Wickersham told the

Dossetter Collection #42300

Metlakatla was a model community on Annette Island built by 800 Tsimshian refugees from British Columbia in 1889. Under the influence of lay missionary William Duncan, the Tsimshians conducted businesses, operated their own sawmill and cannery and established an elementary school. Presently it is the only Indian reservation in Alaska. (AMERICAN MUSEUM OF NATURAL HISTORY)

chiefs that they could have homesteads or reservations, but that in order to survive they must become civilized like the white man. The chiefs told him that neither homesteads nor reservations made sense to them; all they wanted was to be left alone. But that was not to be.

Some areas remain isolated
but disease strikes everywhere

In northern and western Alaska, beyond the reach of the commercial salmon industry, the pace of cultural change was much slower due to the lack of resources attracting the economic interest of the whites. After the collapse of commercial whaling in the 1890s, coastal northwest Alaska experienced little contact with outsiders. Yupiit peoples of the Yukon-Kuskokwim delta and St. Lawrence Island areas never had any true boom and their isolation has allowed them to retain their language and more of their cultural traditions than other Alaskan Native people.

But no Alaska Native groups were able to escape the ravages of disease. Major causes were influenza and tuberculosis. The Native population declined to its lowest point in 1909 when the census recorded 25,331 persons. Poor housing and sanitation plus inadequate medical services resulted in continuing high death rates among Alaska Natives until the 1950s when an extensive campaign by the U.S. Public Health Service eradicated tuberculosis. Also a village aide program was created to train Natives as primary health providers in the villages. The improved health care resulted in a "baby boom" during the late 1950s and 1960s resulting in a rapid population increase.

Statehood and oil bring land issues to a head

World War II brought the next major wave of white immigration to Alaska. The white population increased from 40,006 in 1939 to 94,780 in 1950. Economic decline after World War II set in motion the struggle for statehood, driven fundamentally by Alaska whites desires to control the resources of the territory.

The Alaska Statehood Act was passed in 1958 and provided for the new state to select 108 million of Alaska's 375 million acres. These selections, which often were made over customary and traditional Native lands, galvanized Natives throughout Alaska to organize into regional associations and protest the taking of their lands.

The dilemmas which the new state posed for Alaska Natives led to the formation of the Alaska Federation of Natives (AFN) in 1966 to pursue the struggle for land claims with the federal government. This organization began lobbying Congress and succeeded in convincing Secretary of the Interior Udall to suspend state land selections in 1966 until Native claims had been settled. In 1968, the giant oil discovery on the North

Slope brought the crisis to a head. With Native claims clouding the title to the land, oil development could not proceed. Native, State and oil corporation leaders all wanted the land claims issued solved. The final outcome was the Alaska Native Claims Settlement Act (ANCSA) signed into law by President Nixon on December 18, 1971.

ANCSA becomes unique experiment

ANCSA provided a cash settlement of $962.5 million and 44 million acres distributed to 12 regional and 200 village corporations. Individual Alaskan Natives alive on December 18, 1971 were enrolled in the corporations based on where they were born or lived and were given 100 shares of stock. Most Alaskan Natives are "shareholders" of both a village and regional corporation. Those born after this date did not receive stock directly.

ANCSA also explicitly extinguished all aboriginal hunting and fishing rights, revoked all previous reservations (except the Tsimshian reservation on Metlakatla) and reiterated the continuing "trust" responsibility of the federal government to protect Alaska Natives. Despite extinguishing fishing and hunting rights, Congress declared that it expected the Department of the Interior and the State of Alaska to provide for the "subsistence needs" of Alaska Natives. This has become a major controversy in Alaska between Natives and non-Natives, rural and urban residents.

ANCSA is a unique experiment in settling land claims and establishing institutions for Native American groups. It was intended by Congress to provide a vehicle for economic development and assimilation. But it has been a limited economic success and few Natives wish to be totally assimilated. Few of the regional corporations have been successful while at least two have been faced with bankruptcy and loss of lands. Village corporations have even less chance of surviving. These concerns led to a new movement for tribal recognition and control of lands known as the "tribal sovereignty" movement. This movement is especially strong among the Yupiit of the Yukon-Kuskokwim delta where the concept of a Yupiit Nation has emerged.

Tribal Sovereignty

Alaska Native concerns over the potential loss of ANCSA lands, but also culture and governance, stimulated tribal sovereignty efforts in the 1980s. The aim of the movement was to establish Alaska Native tribal governments, similar to those of American Indians in the continental United States, with jurisdiction over traditional lands, resources and tribal members. The movement, solidified into the Alaska Inter-Tribal Council in the 1990s, has taken a variety of forms and directions over the years. In 1994, Congressional legislation approved the BIA listing of Alaska Native villages with corporations as tribes. In 1998, however, the Supreme Court declared that ANCSA corporation lands could not be governed as tribal lands but did not deter tribal leaders from continuing to pursue their goal. Governor Knowles created a State-Tribal Commission in 2000 to establish a basis for a working relationship between state agencies and Alaska Native tribes. In May 2001, efforts of this commission led to the Millenium Agreement, signed by the governor and many Alaska Native tribal leaders, declaring the state's recognition of and policy of working with Alaska Native tribes. Only time will tell if this agreement signals a new era of positive working relationships.

"Subsistence"

The question of how traditional Alaska Native hunting, fishing and gathering activities (known in Alaska as "subsistence") are to be treated has been a dilemma ever since ANCSA "extinguished" the formal right to those activities by Alaska Natives but directed state and federal agencies to provide for it. Alaska Natives were successful in getting the federal government establish a rural subsistence priority on federal land as part of the 1980 Alaska National Interest Lands Conservation Act (ANILCA). While based on Indian Law, the priority is provided to all rural residents. The act also required that the State of Alaska establish a similar priority or lose its authority to regulate fish and wildlife resources on federal lands. Since 1992, the State has not been in compliance with ANILCA; in 1996, the U.S. government began managing fish and wildlife on federal lands. The lengthy controversy over subsistence in Alaska has not yet been resolved   despite efforts to craft a solution.   Many Alaska Natives have to come to see federal management as more satisfactory than state management of fish and wildlife resources.

Alaska Natives and the future

The three decades since the passage of ANCSA have seen dramatic changes in Alaska Native life. Better health care has allowed Native population to recover to 119,241 as of 2000 but water and sewer systems in many villages continue to be substandard or nonexistent. Improved housing, village schools and gymnasiums, television, computers and the Internet have all become a part of Alaska Native life in the villages and the cities. While population in the villages has increased, a much larger proportion of Alaska Natives live in Anchorage in 2000 (23 percent) than did at the time of ANCSA's passage in 1970 (2.3 percent). These changes have largely been the result of Alaska's oil-driven boom, the Permanent Fund Dividend derived from investment of a portion of the oil wealth, and federal programs. Economic development due to ANCSA has played a modest but important role in this equation.

Perhaps the most significant impact of ANCSA has been its stimulus to political engagement and political leadership by Alaska Native elites. Political relations with the state government continue to be anxious but the engagement of the federal government has assisted in a number of areas.

Through AFN leadership, Alaska Natives have been successful in getting the Alaska congressional delegation to address a number of serious issues such as rural water and sewer, rural power, transportation, and bulk storage for oil through the Denali Commission. In 1994, the Alaska Native Commission, a federally-mandated review board on the impacts of ANCSA, reported on the dimensions of Alaska Native problems and proposed solutions; this has energized Alaska Natives to pursue the mix of traditional values and institutions with contemporary practices best suited to the present circumstances.

Alaska Natives face an array of problems and challenges in the 21st century. Low prices for salmon and weak runs in western Alaska have seriously undermined the subsistence-based economic foundations in several rural regions. Environmental problems created by the *Exxon Valdez* oil spill in Prince William Sound in 1989 continue to plague Gulf of Alaska villages. There are also significant problems associated with cultural change such as alcoholism, drug addiction, heart disease and diabetes from altered diets, high rates of fetal alcohol syndrome, and serious abuse of women and children. Alaska Natives are also incarcerated at disproportionate levels and experience the highest suicide rates in the nation. Despite improvements in earnings, Alaska Natives still dominate the poverty statistics and have the highest unemployment rates in Alaska.

While this is certainly a daunting list of problems, Alaska Natives are facing the issues and seeking solutions. Alaska Natives have not disappeared, retreated or been devastated by the forces of "future shock." Alaska Natives have recognized that centuries old adaptations and values are a foundation on which to build their lives today.

There is little doubt that the pace of cultural change will continue to quicken, producing challenging, new economic and social conditions. The future of Alaska Natives will continue to be heavily influenced by the attitudes and practices of their non-Native neighbors who, through the Congress and the courts, will establish crucial rules under which Alaska Natives will live. But Alaska Natives are engaged, have developed a strong political voice, have retained appropriate cultural values and goals and are ready to battle for a positive future. We all share responsibility for the future of Alaska's Native peoples.

Edward Bovy

Anchorage's Alaska Native Heritage Center is one of many facilities that have opened in recent years. Conceived and operated by several Alaska Native regional corporations, ANHC is dedicated to increasing the understanding and appreciation of Alaska Native cultures.

Epilogue: Alaska Natives and Cultural Heritage

The remarkable material, social and cultural heritage of Alaska Natives has become a central focus of contemporary Alaska Native consciousness. The desire to practice, preserve, repatriate and understand is demonstrated in a wide range of activities by Alaska Natives from the national to the local level.

At the national level, Alaska Natives have been active in the process of repatriating human remains and burial goods as required by federal law. One of the first major repatriation efforts, led by Dr. Gordon Pullar (Koniag Alutiiq), was the return of more than 90 human skeletons by the Smithsonian Institution to the village of Larsen Bay where they were reburied. Another national level cultural heritage activity involving Alaska Natives is the development of the National Museum of the American Indian in front of the capitol in Washington, DC. Dr. Rosita Worl (Tlingit) sits on the board of directors; two Alaska Native groups, the Tlingit and the Yup'ik, will have exhibits devoted to them at the opening of the facility in 2004.

Two statewide initiatives of note are the Alaska Native Heritage Center and Youth-Elder Conferences of the Alaska Federation of Natives. The Alaska Native Heritage Center (ANHC) is a combination educational and cultural center located in Anchorage that is funded by a consortium of Alaska Native regional corporations. The ANHC, which opened in 1998, stages exhibits, meetings, and cultural events but is best known for its replicas of housing structures from six Alaska Native groups that are located around a man-made lake on the center grounds. The AFN has made it a priority to bridge the generational gap by bringing the youth and elders together as part of the annual statewide convention held in Anchorage each October.

One of the most successful examples of direct Alaska Native engagement with research, cultural preservation, cultural representation and cultural education at the regional level is the Alutiiq Museum which opened in Kodiak in 2000. The effort to obtain a museum by the Koniag was initiated in the mid-1980s based on the abundant and exquisite artifacts emerging from the archeological excavations at Karluk Lagoon. A repository complete with state-of-the-art temperature and air controls was made possible by funding from the *Exxon Valdez* Trust Fund. Dr. Sven Haakanson, a Koniag Alutiiq from Old Harbor earned a doctorate in anthropology from Harvard University and is the director of the Museum. In addition to his active engagement in research Dr. Haakanson also has made a powerful impact on education by developing and implementing mask, baidarka, and artifact-making classes in Kodiak area schools.

Collaboration between anthropologists, museologists and Alaska Native experts has become the norm in the production of museum exhibits. Perhaps the most stunning display to date was the *Agaliyarput* production that brought together masks from collections all over the world along with accounts of the masks and demonstrations of the central Yup'ik song and dance that gave life to the masks. Marie Meade (Yup'ik) collected, translated and published oral traditions provided by Central Yup'ik elders of masks and dances they recalled.

Even local groups have become actively involved in cultural heritage projects. The Huna Heritage Foundation, for example, has staged highly successful Clan Conferences for more than a decade. These well-attended events provide training in cultural knowledge and ceremonial protocol as elders provide instruction, recount oral traditions, and answer questions.

Through these and many other activities, Alaska Natives are continuing and strengthening their rich cultural heritage.

Selected Museums and Cultural Centers

ANAKTUVUK PASS

Simon Paneak Memorial Museum
341 Mekiana Road
PO Box 21085
Anaktuvuk Pass, AK 99721
(907) 661-3413; fax 661-3414
www.nsbsd.k12.ak.us/villages/akp/
museum/panintro.htm
NUNAMIUT ESKIMO HISTORY AND TRADITIONS

ANCHORAGE

Alaska Native Heritage Center
8800 Heritage Center Dr.
Anchorage, AK 99506
(907) 330-8000
www.alaskanative.net
*Workshops, demonstrations and
guided tours of indoor exhibits and
outdoor village sites*

Anchorage Museum of History & Art
121 West 7th Avenue
PO Box 196650
Anchorage, AK 99519-6650
(907) 343-4326; fax 343-6149
www.anchoragemuseum.org
*Exhibits and collections represent
Alaska's Natives, state history, and
Alaskan art*

ANVIK

Anvik Historical Society and Museum
PO Box 110, Anvik, AK 99558
(907) 663-6358
*Local Athabaskan artifacts from mid-
19th century to the present*

BARROW

Inupiat Heritage Center
Ilisagvik College
Barrow, AK 99723
(800)-478-7337; fax 852-1752

*Exhibits, collections, educational
outreach, performances and
activities, meeting rooms, Qargi,
library*

BETHEL

Yupiit Piciryarait Cultural Center
and Museum
420 Chief Eddie Hoffman Highway
PO Box 219, Bethel, AK 99559
(907) 543-1819; fax 543-1885
*Clothing, household, hunting and
gathering implements used by the
people of the Yukon-Kuskokwim
Delta in ancient and contemporary
times*

CORDOVA

Cordova Historical Museum
622 First Street
PO Box 391, Cordova, AK 99574
(907) 424-6665; fax 424-6666

DILLINGHAM

Samuel K. Fox Museum
Corner of Seward & D Streets
PO Box 330, Dillingham, AK 99576
(907) 842-5115
*Large collection of Central Yup'ik
objects including carvings and
baskets; skin sewing & fur exhibit*

EKLUTNA

Eklutna Historical Park
16515 Centerfield Drive, # 201
Eagle River, AK 99577
(907) 696-2828; fax 696-2845
www.alaskaone.com/eklutna
*Dena'ina Athabascan Indians
historical exhibits and Native art;
St. Nicholas Russian Orthodox
Church and the Eklutna Cemetery,*

*known for its colorfully decorated
"spirit houses."*

FAIRBANKS

Alaska Native Village Museum
Alaskaland Park
201 First Avenue, Suite 200,
Fairbanks, AK 99701
(907) 452-1648
*Contemporary collection of
Athabaskan cultural materials*

Univ. of Alaska Fairbanks Museum
907 Yukon Drive
PO Box 756960, Fairbanks, AK
99775-6960
(907) 474-7505; fax 474-5469
www.uaf.edu/museum/index.html
*Collections in aquatics, archeology,
earth sciences, ethnology, herbarium,
history*

HAINES

Alaska Indian Arts
#23 Fort Seward Drive
PO Box 271, Haines, AK 99827
(907) 766-2160; fax 766-2105
*Chilkat dancers; totem carving,
silkscreen and silver carving with
Native artists; Tlingit artifacts*

Sheldon Museum & Cultural Center
Main & First Streets
PO Box 269, Haines, AK 99827
(907) 766-2366; fax 766-2368
www.sheldonmuseum.org
Art and culture of Native Tlingit people

HOMER

Pratt Museum
3779 Bartlett St., Homer, AK 99603
(907) 235-8635; fax 235-2764
www.prattmuseum.org
*Natural and cultural history of the
Kenai Peninsula*

HUSLIA

Huslia Cultural Center
PO Box 70, Huslia, AK 99746
(907) 829-2256
Athabaskan sleds and clothing

JUNEAU

Alaska State Museum
395 Whittier St., Juneau, AK 99801
(907) 465-2901; fax: 465-2976
www.museums.state.ak.us
*Extensive exhibits on the cultures of
Alaska's Native people*

KENAI

Kenai Visitors & Cultural Center
11471 Kenai Spur Highway
Kenai, AK 99611
(907) 283-1991; fax 283-2230
www.visitkenai.com
*Athabaskan, Aleut and Russian
cultural exhibits*

KETCHIKAN

Southeast Alaska Visitor Center
USDA Forest Service
50 Main Street, Ketchikan, AK 99901
(907) 228-6214; fax 228-6234
www.nps.gov/aplic/
*Tsimshian, Haida and Tlingit totem
poles, rainforest room*

Totem Heritage Center
601 Deermont St.
Ketchikan, AK 99901
(907) 225-5900; fax 225-5602
www.city.ketchikan.ak.us/ds/
tonghert/index.html
*World-renowned collection of original,
unrestored 19th century totem poles
retrieved from abandoned Native
villages near Ketchikan. Additional
exhibits illuminate the rich culture of
the Tlingit, Haida and Tsimshian*

KODIAK

Alutiiq Museum
215 Mission Road, Suite 101
Kodiak, AK 99615
(907) 486-7004; fax 486-7048
www.alutiiqmuseum.com
*Prehistoric and historic traditions of
the Alutiiq; large collection of Alutiiq
artifacts*

Baranov Museum
101 Marine Way, Kodiak, AK 99615
(907) 486-5920; fax 486-3166
www.ptialaska.net/~baranov
*Historical objects from the Aleutian
Islands and the Kodiak Archipelago*

PETERSBURG

Clausen Memorial Museum
203 Fram Street
PO Box 708, Petersburg, AK 99833
(907) 772-3598
Tlingit canoe

SITKA

Isabel Miller Museum
330 Harbor Drive, Sitka, AK 99835
(907) 747-6455; fax 747-6588
www.sitka.org/historicalmuseum/
*Collection of Tlingit, Russian and local
hand-crafted items*

Sitka National Historical Park
106 Metlakatla Street
PO Box 738, Sitka, AK 99835
(907) 747-6281; fax 747-5938
http://www.nps.gov/sitk/
*Extensive collection of historic Tlingit
and Haida totem poles; also houses
the Southeast Alaska Indian Cultural
Center, Inc., an independent organization of Tlingit artists who demonstrate
traditional wood and silver carving*

UNALASKA

Museum of the Aleutians
PO Box 648, Unalaska, AK 99685
(907) 581-5150
www.aleutians.org
*Aleut/Unangan prehistory and
ethnographic items*

VALDEZ

Alaska Cultural Center
300 Airport Road, Valdez Airport
Terminal
PO Box 97, Valdez, AK 99686
(907) 834-1690; fax 835-8933
*Large collection of Native artifacts,
dolls, beadwork, baskets, masks*

Valdez Museum
217 Egan Drive
PO Box 8, Valdez, AK 99686
(907) 835-2764 or 835-5800
www.alaska.net/~vldzmuse/
index.html

WRANGELL

Tribal House of the Bear
foot of Front Street
PO Box 868, Wrangell, AK 99929
(907) 874-3747
Replica of a traditional tribal house

Wrangell Museum
318 Church Street
PO Box 1050, Wrangell, AK 99929
(907) 874-3770; fax 874-3785
www.wrangell.com/cultural/
museum.htm
*Original house posts from Chief
Shakes house carved in the mid-
1700s, a "spruce canoe," a turn-of-
the-century spruce and cedar bark
basket collection, several original
totem poles*

References and Additional Reading

Chapter 1: Introduction

Damas, David (ed.). 1984. *Handbook of North American Indians, Vol. 5; Arctic.*
    Washington D.C.: Smithsonian Institution.
Dumond, Donald. 1977. *The Eskimos and Aleuts.* London: Thames and Hudson.
Fitzhugh, William and Crowell, Aron (eds.) 1988. *Crossroads of Continents: Cultures of
    Siberia and Alaska.* Washington, D.C.: Smithsonian Institution .
Helm, June (ed.). 1981. *Handbook of North American Indians, Vol. 6: Subarctic.*
    Washington D.C.: Smithsonian Institution.
Suttles, Wayne (ed.). 1990. *Handbook of North American Indians, Vol. 7: Northwest Coast.*
    Washington, D. C.: Smithsonian Institution.
West, Frederick Hadleigh (ed.). 1996. *American Beginnings: The Prehistory and Paleoecology
    of Beringia.* Chicago: University of Chicago Press.

Chapter 2: Unangan/Aleut

Black, Lydia. 1980. Early History. *In* The Aleutians, L. Morgan (ed.). *Alaska Geographic*
    7(3): 82-105.
Black, Lydia. 1982. *Aleut Art.* Anchorage: The Aleutian /Pribilof Island Association.
Black, Lydia. 1991. *Glory Remembered: Wooden Headgear of Alaska Sea Hunters.* Juneau:
    Alaska State Museums.
Lantis, Margaret. 1984. Aleut. *In* Damas, D. (ed.). *Handbook of North American Indians,
    Vol. 5: Arctic.* pp. 161-184.
Laughlin, William. 1980. *Aleuts: Survivors of the Bering Land Bridge.* New York;
    Holt, Rinehart and Winston.

Chapter 3: Sugpiaq/Alutiiq (Pacific Eskimos)

Clark, Donald. 1984. Pacific Eskimo: Historical Ethnography. *In* Damas, D. (ed.).
    Handbook of North American Indians, Vol. 5: Arctic. pp. 185-197.
Crowell, Aron, Amy Steffian and Gordon L. Pullar (eds.) 2001. *Looking Both Ways:
    Heritage and Identity of the Alutiiq People.* Fairbanks: University of Alaska Press.
Fitzhugh, William and Chaussonet, Valerie (eds.) 1994. *Anthropology of the North Pacific
    Rim.* Washington, D.C.: Smithsonian Institution.
Johnson, John (compiler). 1984. *Chugach Legends: Stories and Photographs of the Chugach
    Region.* Anchorage: Chugach Alaska Corporation.
Zimmerly, David. 1986. *Qajak: Kayaks of Siberia and Alaska.* Juneau: Alaska State
    Museums.

Chapter 4: Yupiit (Bering Sea Eskimos)

Barker, James. 1993. *Always Getting Ready, Upterrlainarluta: Yup'ik Eskimo Subsistence
    in Southwest Alaska.* Seattle: University of Washington Press.

Fienup-Riordan, Ann. 1983. *The Nelson Island Eskimo*. Anchorage: Alaska Pacific
    University Press.
Fienup-Riordan, Ann. 1994. *Boundaries and Passages: Rule and Ritual in Yup'ik Oral
    Tradition*. Norman: University of Oklahoma Press.
Fitzhugh, William and Kaplan, Susan. 1982. *Inua: Spirit World of the Bering Sea Eskimo*.
    Washington, D. C.: Smithsonian Institution.
Hughes, Charles. 1984. Saint Lawrence Island Eskimo. *In* Damas, D. (ed.). *Handbook of
    North American Indians, Vol. 5: Arctic*. pp. 262-277.
Meade, Marie (translater) and Fienup-Riordan, Ann (ed.) 1996. *Agayuliyararput,Our Way of
    Making Prayer- Yup'ik Masks and the Stories They Tell*. Anchorage: Anchorage Museum
    of History and Art.
Oswalt, Wendell. 1990. *Bashful No Longer: An Alaska Eskimo Ethnohistory, 1788-1988*.
    Norman: University of Oklahoma Press.
Silook, Susie. 2001. Inupiaq and Yupik People of Alaska. *Alaska Geographic* 28(3)
Van Stone, James. 1984. Mainland Southwest Alaska Eskimo. *In* Damas, D. (ed.).
    Handbook of North American Indians, Vol 5: Arctic. pp. 224-242.

Chapter 5: Inupiat (Northern Eskimos)

Burch, Ernest. 1984. Kotzebue Sound Eskimo. *In* Damas, D.(ed.). *Handbook of North
    American Indians, Vol. 5: Arctic*. pp. 303-319.
Burch, Ernest. 1998. *The Inupiaq Eskimo Nations of Northwest Alaska*. Fairbanks:
    University of Alaska Press.
Campbell, John. 1998. *North Alaska Chronicle: Notes from the End of Time*. Santa Fe:
    Museum of New Mexico Press.
Chance, Norman. 1990. *The Inupiat of Northern Alaska: An Ethnography of Development*.
    New York: Holt, Rinehart and Winston.
Hall, Edward. 1984. Interior North Alaska Eskimos. *In* Damas, D. (ed.). *Handbook of North
    American Indians, Vol. 5: Arctic*. pp. 338-346.
Hess, Bill. 1999. *Gift of the Whale: The Inupiat Bowhead Hunt, a Sacred Tradition*.
    Vancouver: Sasquatch Books.
Jorgensen, Joseph. 1990. *Oil Age Eskimos*. Berkeley: University of California Press.
Oswalt, Wendell. 1967. *Alaskan Eskimos*. Scranton, Pennsylvania: Chandler Publishing
    Company.

Chapter 6: Athabaskans (Interior Indians)

Herbert, Belle. 1982. *Shandaa: In My Life Time*. Fairbanks: Alaska Native Language Center,
    University of Alaska Anchorage.
Nelson, Richard. 1983a. *Make Prayers to the Raven: A Koyukon View of the Northern Forest*
    Chicago: University of Chicago Press.
Nelson, Richard. 1983b. *The Athabascans: People of the Boreal Forest*. Fairbanks:
    University of Alaska Museum.
Simeone, William. 1982. *A History of Alaskan Athapaskans*. Anchorage: Alaska Historical
    Commission.
Simpson, Ronald. 2001. *The Legacy of Chief Nicolai*. Anchorage: Publication Consultants.

Slobodin, James. 1981. Kutchin. *In* Helm, J. (ed.). *Handbook of North American Indians,*
    Vol. 6: Subarctic. pp. 514-532.
Van Stone, James. 1974. *Athapaskan Adaptations.* Chicago: Aldine Publishing Company.

Chapter 7: Tlingit and Haida (Southeast Coastal Indians)

Brown, Steve. 1998. *Native Visions: Northwest Coast Art, 18th Century to the Present.*
    Seattle: Seattle Art Museum.
Dauenhauer, Richard and Nora (eds.). 1994. *Haa Kooteeya, Our Culture: Tlingit Life Stories.*
    Seattle: University of Washington Press.
Emmons, George. 1991. *The Tlingit.* Seattle: University of Washington Press.
Jonaitis, Aldona. 1986. *The Art of the Northern Tlingit.* Seattle: University of
    Washington Press.
Kan, Sergei. 1989. *Symbolic Immortality.* Washington, D.C.: Smithsonian Institution Press.
Oberg, Kalervo. 1973. *The Social Economy of the Tlingit Indians.* Seattle: University of
    Washington Press.
Olson, Wallace. 1991. *The Tlingit: An Introduction to Their Culture and History.*
    Auke Bay, Alaska: Heritage Research.
Thornton, Thomas (ed.) 2000. *Haa Aani, Our Land.* Seattle: University of Washington Press.

Chapter 8: Historic Change

Arnold, Robert et al. 1976. *Alaska Native Land Claims.* Anchorage: Alaska Native Foundation.
Berger, Thomas. 1985. *Village Journey.* New York: Hill and Wang.
Black, Lydia. 2002. *Russians in Alaska, 1741-1867.* Fairbanks: University of Alaska Press.
Case, David. 1984. *Alaska Natives and American Laws.* Fairbanks: University of Alaska Press.
Dauenhauer, Richard L. 1997 *Conflicting Visions in Alaskan Education.* Fairbanks:
    University of Alaska.
Fortuine, Robert. 1989. *Chills and Fever: Health and Disease in the Early History of Alaska.*
    Fairbanks: University of Alaska Press.
Hinckley, Ted. 1972. *The Americanization of Alaska, 1867-1897.* Palo Alto, California:
    Pacific Books.
Jones, Dorothy. 1980. *A Century of Servitude: Pribilof Aleuts under U.S. Rule.*
    University Press of America.
McMurray, Peter. 1985. *The Devil and Mr. Duncan: A History of the Two Metlakatlas.*
    Victoria: Sono Nis Press.
Ray, Dorothy Jean. 1992. *The Eskimos about Bering Strait, 1650-1898.* Seattle:
    University of Washington Press.
Smith, Barbara S. and Redmond J. Barnett (eds.). 1990. *Russian America: The*
    Forgotten Frontier. Tacoma: Washington State Historical Society.

An impressive and important website entitled the Alaska Native Knowledge Network has been
created by Alaska Native cultural leaders and educators to provide accurate information about
Alaska Natives. The website address is: www.ankn.uaf.edu